FIRST WORD
LAST WORD
GOD'S WORD
VOLUME TWO

Titles in the Seedbed Daily Text series:

The Advent Mission: Advent by Omar Rikabi
Behold, the Man: John by J. D. Walt
Between You and Me: 2 John, 3 John, Philemon, Titus, and Jude by Omar Rikabi
But Encourage One Another Daily as Long as It Is Called Today by J. D. Walt
The Christian New Year: Advent by J. D. Walt
The Domino Effect: Colossians by J. D. Walt
First Love: Philippians by J. D. Walt
The First Real Christian: James by J. D. Walt
First Word. Last Word. God's Word: The Bible by J. D. Walt
First Word. Last Word. God's Word Vol. 2: The Bible by J. D. Walt
God Is Here: Advent by Casey Page Culbreth
The Gospel of the Holy Spirit: Mark by J. D. Walt
Listen to Him: Lent by J. D. Walt
People Who Say Such Things: Faith by J. D. Walt
Protagonist: Advent by Matt LeRoy and Josh LeRoy
Reset: Advent by J. D. Walt
Right Here, Right Now, Jesus: Prayer by J. D. Walt
Soundtrack: Lent by J. D. Walt
This Is How We Know: 1 John by J. D. Walt
(un)Puzzled: Ephesians by J. D. Walt
What Happens in Corinth: 1 Corinthians by J. D. Walt
Wilderness: Exodus by J. D. Walt

FIRST WORD
LAST WORD
GOD'S WORD
VOLUME TWO

The Bible

J. D. WALT

Copyright 2022 by J. D. Walt

All rights reserved. No part of this publication may be reproduced, stored in a retrieval system, or transmitted, in any form or by any means—electronic, mechanical, photocopying, recording, or otherwise—without prior written permission, except for brief quotations in critical reviews or articles.

Scripture quotations are taken from the Holy Bible, New International Version®, NIV® Copyright © 1973, 1978, 1984, 2011 by Biblica, Inc.™ Used by permission of Zondervan. All rights reserved worldwide. www.zondervan.com The "NIV" and "New International Version" are trademarks registered in the United States Patent and Trademark Office by Biblica, Inc.™ All rights reserved worldwide.

Scripture quotations marked MSG are taken from *THE MESSAGE*, copyright © 1993, 1994, 1995, 1996, 2000, 2001, 2002 by Eugene H. Peterson. Used by permission of NavPress. All rights reserved. Represented by Tyndale House Publishers, Inc.

Scripture quotations marked ESV are from the ESV® Bible (The Holy Bible, English Standard Version®), copyright © 2001 by Crossway, a publishing ministry of Good News Publishers. Used by permission. All rights reserved.

Printed in the United States of America

Cover and page design by Strange Last Name
Page layout by PerfecType, Nashville, Tennessee

Walt, J. D. (John David)
  First word, last word, God's word : the Bible / J.D. Walt. – Franklin, Tennessee : Seedbed Publishing, ©2020-2022.

   2 volumes ; 18 cm. – (Seedbed daily text)

   ISBN: 9781628247930 (v.1 ; paperback) – 9781628249668 (v.2 ; paperback)
   ISBN: 9781628247947 (v.1 ; Mobi) – 9781628249675 (v.2 ; Mobi)
   ISBN: 9781628247954 (v.1 ; ePub) – 9781628249682 (v.2 ; ePub)
   ISBN: 9781628247961 (v.1 ; uPDF) – 9781628249699 (v.2 ; uPDF)
   OCLC: 1235782658

   1. Bible--Evidences, authority, etc.--Meditations. 2. Bible--Inspiration--Mediations. 3. Spiritual exercises. I. Title. II. Series.

BS480.W34 2020   220.1/3   2020940079

SEEDBED PUBLISHING
Franklin, Tennessee
seedbed.com

Contents

	An Invitation to Awakening	vii
	How the Daily Text Works	xi
1.	The Greatest Sermon Ever Preached	3
2.	When E. F. Hutton Talks . . .	4
3.	Do You Read Me?	8
4.	Have You Found God's Word for the Year?	11
5.	What Is Your First Word Every Day? How about Your Last Word?	14
6.	My First Word—Last Word—God's Word	16
7.	Moving from the Extraction Approach to the Immersion Approach	19
8.	Carpool Catechesis	22
9.	Morning, Coffee, and the Word of God	25
10.	God's Way: Perfect. God's Word: Flawless.	27
11.	Shower Words	31
12.	On the Source and Other Sources	34
13.	The Word Is Not Magic, but It Is Miraculous	37
14.	The Simple and Comprehensive Invitation of the Word of God	40
15.	Enlarging Our Vision of the Word of God	43
16.	Learning to Anchor in the Word of God	45
17.	Anchor Buddies	49
18.	Keeping Our Eye on the Ball of the Word of God	52

19.	How God's Word Designs the World It Declares	56
20.	17:17 My New Double Domino	59
21.	Turn on Your Lights!	61
22.	Learning Scripture like Language	64
23.	The Wonderful Way of Immersion in the Word of God	68
24.	Formed by the Word, Filled by the Spirit	70
25.	Trading Our Assumptions for God's Assurances	74
26.	Calling for a Verdict	77
27.	How I Got My House Back	80
28.	When the Word of God Asks Us a Question (Question 1 of 3)	83
29.	When the Word of God Asks Us a Question (Question 2 of 3)	86
30.	When the Word of God Asks Us a Question (Question 3 of 3)	90
The Sower's Creed		94

An Invitation to Awakening

This resource comes with an invitation.

The invitation is as simple as it is comprehensive. It is not an invitation to commit your life to this or that cause or to join an organization or to purchase another book. The invitation is this: to wake up to the life you always hoped was possible and the reason you were put on planet Earth.

It begins with following Jesus Christ. In case you are unaware, Jesus was born in the first century BCE into a poor family from Nazareth, a small village located in what is modern-day Israel. While his birth was associated with extraordinary phenomena, we know little about his childhood. At approximately thirty years of age, Jesus began a public mission of preaching, teaching, and healing throughout the region known as Galilee. His mission was characterized by miraculous signs and wonders; extravagant care of the poor and marginalized; and multiple unconventional claims about his own identity and purpose. In short, he claimed to be the incarnate Son of God with the mission and power to save people from sin, deliver them from death, and bring them into the now and eternal kingdom of God—on earth as it is in heaven.

In the spring of his thirty-third year, during the Jewish Passover celebration, Jesus was arrested by the religious authorities, put on trial in the middle of the night, and at their urging, sentenced to death by a Roman governor. On the day known to history as Good Friday, Jesus was crucified on a Roman cross. He was buried in a borrowed tomb. On the following Sunday, according to multiple eyewitness accounts, he was physically raised from the dead. He appeared to hundreds of people, taught his disciples, and prepared for what was to come.

Forty days after the resurrection, Jesus ascended bodily into the heavens where, according to the Bible, he sits at the right hand of God, as the Lord of heaven and earth. Ten days after his ascension, in a gathering of 120 people on the day of Pentecost, a Jewish day of celebration, something truly extraordinary happened. A loud and powerful wind swept over the people gathered. Pillars of what appeared to be fire descended upon the followers of Jesus. The Holy Spirit, the presence and power of God, filled the people, and the church was born. After this, the followers of Jesus went forth and began to do the very things Jesus did—preaching, teaching, and healing—planting churches and making disciples all over the world. Today, more than two thousand years later, the movement has reached us. This is the Great Awakening and it has never stopped.

Yes, two thousand years hence and more than two billion followers of Jesus later, this awakening movement of Jesus Christ and his church stands stronger than ever. Billions of ordinary people the world over have discovered in Jesus Christ an awakened life they never imagined possible. They have overcome challenges, defeated addictions, endured untenable hardships and suffering with unexplainable joy, and stared death in the face with the joyful confidence of eternal life. They have healed the sick, gathered the outcasts, embraced the oppressed, loved the poor, contended for justice, labored for peace, cared for the dying and, yes, even raised the dead.

We all face many challenges and problems. They are deeply personal, yet when joined together, they create enormous and complex chaos in the world, from our hearts to our homes to our churches and our cities. All of this chaos traces to two originating problems: sin and death. Sin, far beyond mere moral failure, describes the fundamental broken condition of every human being. Sin separates us from God and others, distorts and destroys our deepest identity as the image-bearers of God, and poses a fatal problem from which we cannot save ourselves. It results in an ever-diminishing quality of life and ultimately ends in eternal death. Because Jesus lived a life of sinless perfection, he is able to save us from sin and restore us to a right relationship with God, others, and ourselves. He did this through his sacrificial death on the cross on our behalf. Because Jesus rose from the dead, he is able to deliver us from death and bring us into a quality of life both eternal and unending.

This is the gospel of Jesus Christ: pardon from the penalty of sin, freedom from the power of sin, deliverance from the grip of death, and awakening to the supernatural empowerment of the Holy Spirit to live powerfully for the good of others and the glory of God. Jesus asks only that we acknowledge our broken selves as failed sinners, trust him as our Savior, and follow him as our Lord. Following Jesus does not mean an easy life; however, it does lead to a life of power and purpose, joy in the face of suffering, and profound, even world-changing, love for God and people.

All of this is admittedly a lot to take in. Remember, this is an invitation. Will you follow Jesus? Don't let the failings of his followers deter you. Come and see for yourself.

Here's a prayer to get you started:

> Our Father in heaven, it's me (say your name), I want to know you. I want to live an awakened life. I confess I am a sinner. I have failed myself, others, and you in many ways. I know you made me for a purpose and I want to fulfill that purpose with my one life. I want to follow Jesus Christ. Jesus, thank you for the gift of your life and death and resurrection and ascension on my behalf. I want to walk in relationship with you as Savior and Lord. Would you lead me into the fullness and newness of life I was made for? I am ready to follow you. Come, Holy Spirit, and fill me with the love, power, and purposes of God. I pray these things by faith in the name of Jesus, amen.

It would be our privilege to help you get started and grow deeper in this awakened life of following Jesus. For some next steps and encouragements visit seedbed.com/awaken.

How the Daily Text Works

It seems obvious to say, but the Daily Text is written every day. Mostly it is written the day before it is scheduled to release online.

Before you read further, you are cordially invited to subscribe to and receive the daily e-mail. Visit seedbed.com/dailytext to get started. Also, check out the popular Facebook group, Seedbed Daily Text.

Eventually, the daily postings become part of a Daily Text discipleship resource. That's what you hold in your hands now.

It's not exactly a Bible study, though the Bible is both the source and subject. You will learn something about the Bible along the way: its history, context, original languages, and authors. The goal is not educational in nature, but transformational. Seedbed is more interested in folks knowing Jesus than knowing *about* Jesus.

To that end, each reading begins with the definitive inspiration of the Holy Spirit, the ongoing, unfolding text of Scripture. Following that is a short and, hopefully, substantive insight from the text and some aspect of its meaning. For insight to lead to deeper influence, we turn the text into prayer. Finally, influence must run its course toward impact. This is why we ask each other questions. These questions are not designed to elicit information but to crystallize intention.

Discipleship always leads from inspiration to intention and from attention to action.

Using the Daily Text as a Discipleship Curricular Resource for Groups

While Scripture always addresses us personally, it is not written to us individually. The content of Scripture cries out for a community to address. The Daily Text is made for discipleship in community. This resource can work in several different ways. It could be read like a traditional book, a few pages or chapters at a time. Though unadvisable, the readings could be crammed in on the night before the meeting. Keep in mind, the Daily Text is not called the Daily Text for kicks. We believe Scripture is worthy of our most focused and consistent attention. Every day. We all have misses, but let's make every day more than a noble aspiration. Let's make it our covenant with one another.

For Use with Bands

In our judgment, the best and highest use of the Daily Text is made through what we call banded discipleship. A band is a same-gender group of three to five people who read together, pray together, and meet together to become the love of God for one another and the world. With banded discipleship, the daily readings serve more as a common text for the band and grist for the interpersonal conversation mill between meetings. The band meeting is reserved for the specialized activities of high-bar discipleship.

To learn more about bands and banded discipleship, visit discipleshipbands.com. Be sure to download the free *Discipleship Bands: A Practical Field Guide* or order a supply of the printed booklets online. Also be sure to explore Discipleship Bands, our native app designed specifically for the practice of banded discipleship, in the App Store or Google Play.

For Use with Classes and Small Groups

The Daily Text has also proven to be a helpful discipleship resource for a variety of small groups, from community groups to Sunday school classes. Here are some suggested guidelines for deploying the Daily Text as a resource for a small group or class setting:

1. Hearing the Text

Invite the group to settle into silence for a period of no less than one and no more than five minutes. Ask an appointed person to keep time and to read the biblical text covering the period of days since the last group meeting. Allow at least one minute of silence following the reading of the text.

2. Responding to the Text

Invite anyone from the group to respond to the reading by answering these prompts: What did you hear? What did you see? What did you otherwise sense from the Lord?

3. Sharing Insights and Implications for Discipleship

Moving in an orderly rotation (or free-for-all), invite people to share insights and implications from the week's readings.

What did you find challenging, encouraging, provocative, comforting, invasive, inspiring, corrective, affirming, guiding, or warning? Allow group conversation to proceed at will. Limit to one sharing item per turn, with multiple rounds of discussion.

4. Shaping Intentions for Prayer

Invite each person in the group to share a single discipleship intention for the week ahead. It is helpful if the intention can also be framed as a question the group can use to check in from the prior week. At each person's turn, he or she is invited to share how their intention went during the previous week. The class or group can open and close their meeting according to their established patterns.

FIRST WORD
LAST WORD
GOD'S WORD
VOLUME TWO

The Greatest Sermon Ever Preached

ISAIAH 40:8 | The grass withers and the flowers fall,
but the word of our God endures forever.

Consider This

Some years ago, a fascinating incident happened at one of the largest Christian conferences in the country. A well-known, young, revolutionary-type preacher was invited as one of a dozen or so keynote speakers. The young man's participation in the conference generated great anticipation and excitement and undoubtedly accounted for enhanced ticket sales. The moment came for him to give his talk. He stepped to the pulpit amid great adulation, and the large crowd fell silent. He told the gathering they were about to hear the greatest sermon ever preached. Then he opened his Bible and turned to Matthew 5. He read the whole chapter. Then he read all of chapter 6 and following that all of chapter 7. Then he closed his Bible and quietly walked off the stage. It took all of eighteen minutes; far less than the standard fare of forty-five-minute to an hour-long conference talks.

You will recognize this text as the Sermon on the Mount—the greatest sermon ever preached—proclaimed by Jesus Messiah, the Son of God himself.

Here's the interesting thing. Most of the people were quite disappointed, even upset, with the preacher. Though he spoke not one original word, no one there will ever forget what he said. Though he was one of a dozen celebrated speakers, no one remembers any of them or their talks; only his. Though the story has been told now ten thousand times, no one ever quite remembers the name of the conference or anything else about it—only these eighteen minutes of a two-thousand-year-old sermon.

The Prayer

Yes, Lord, we have invested quite heavily in the grass and the flowers and all they represent in this life. We have bought a lot of stock in the things that will only wither and fade. Awaken us afresh to the Word of our God—who alone will endure forever. We are weary of saluting you. We are ready to surrender. In Jesus' name, amen.

The Questions

- Are you ready for less withering grass and fading flowers and more of the forever enduring Word of God? How might we actualize such a priority going forward?

2 When E. F. Hutton Talks . . .

MATTHEW 7:24–27 | "Therefore everyone who hears these words of mine and puts them into practice is like a wise man who built his house on the rock. The rain came down, the streams rose, and the winds blew and beat against that house; yet it did not fall, because it had its foundation on the rock. But everyone who hears these words of mine and does not put them into practice is like a foolish man who built his house on sand. The rain came down, the streams rose, and the winds blew and beat against that house, and it fell with a great crash."

Consider This

Some of you will no doubt remember the famous Wall Street brokerage house known as E. F. Hutton. We remember it from the famous catchphrase on their 1980s-era television commercials: "When E. F. Hutton talks . . . people listen." We don't hear much about E. F. Hutton anymore. It kind of reminds me of the greatest catchphrase of all time: "The grass withers and the flowers fall, but the word of our God endures forever" (Isa. 40:8).

That's the big point of today's text, isn't it? When Jesus talks . . . people listen . . . or they don't. In these closing words of the most famous sermon ever given (a.k.a. the Sermon on the Mount), Jesus gives us two home-building packages. And these aren't spec homes. They are custom homes. Though there be a thousand choices in the building of this home, only one choice ultimately matters. That choice is the foundation on which the house is built. We can choose to build our house on the firm foundation of the rock or on the shifting sediment of the sand. Only it turns out this is not really the choice at all. After all, who would willingly choose to build their house on a foundation of sand, right? The real choice is whether to listen to his words and put them into practice or to listen and not put them into practice. We will choose one or the other. There is no middle way. The choice we make with respect to the words of Jesus determines the outcome of the house we build.

In case "The grass withers and the flowers fall, but the word of our God endures forever" wasn't clear enough, Jesus wants to make it even plainer: you pick the floor plan. You choose the building materials. Make it as spartan or spectacular as you want. It matters not. There are two guarantees. Guarantee #1: Storms will come against your house. Guarantee #2: The foundation will determine its future. The Taj Mahal built on a foundation of shifting sand will fall with a great crash. The most humble shanty built on the firm foundation of the impregnable fortress of the Word of God will endure forever.

"The grass withers and the flowers fall, but the word of our God endures forever" (Isa. 40:8).

So whatever happened to E. F. Hutton? Why doesn't anyone listen to E. F. Hutton anymore? There is a supreme irony afoot here. It turns out through a sustained series of more than two thousand fraudulent banking transactions—most of them small—they lost their way, and their business. And that sound we hear? It's not the echo of E. F. Hutton's words, but the eternally reverberating words of Jesus: *"But everyone who hears these words of mine and does not put them into practice is like a foolish man who built his house on sand. The rain came down, the streams rose, and the winds blew and beat against that house, and it fell with a great crash."*

And that harrowingly loud crashing sound of an implosion? That's E. F. Hutton's house collapsing into the sand.

The Prayer

Yes, Lord, we want to build our lives on the foundation of your Word. And yet we wonder, will it take a storm to reveal the foundation on which we have built? Would you awaken us to the Word of God, beyond the ways we have known or experienced before? We sense a new readiness in our souls, a deeper sensitivity to something you want to sow deep into the soil of our hearts. Thank you for your Word, written down on scrolls and wrapped in the human flesh of your Son. In Jesus' name, amen.

The Questions

- When is the last time you seriously contemplated cheating on your taxes? Or fudging in a business deal to your own advantage? Or trying to reframe the rules or slightly bend them to help your cause? Or your children's? When we aren't listening to Jesus and putting his Word into practice, whose words are we listening to and practicing? Friendly reminder: It's never worth it.

3 Do You Read Me?

MATTHEW 7:24–27 | **"Therefore everyone who hears these words of mine and puts them into practice is like a wise man who built his house on the rock. The rain came down, the streams rose, and the winds blew and beat against that house; yet it did not fall, because it had its foundation on the rock. But everyone who hears these words of mine and does not put them into practice is like a foolish man who built his house on sand. The rain came down, the streams rose, and the winds blew and beat against that house, and it fell with a great crash."**

Consider This

Growing up on the farm in south Arkansas, in the Stone Age preceding cell phones, all our farm trucks had Motorola two-way radios. Each had a unit number. Peepaw was Unit 1, Uncle Martin—Unit 2, Dad—Unit 3, Mr. Eldon (the mechanic)—Unit 4, and the crew—Unit 5. Unit 2 would say, "Come in, Unit 3," and with an affirmative response, Unit 2 would deliver his message. These radios were really just sophisticated walkie-talkies. The lines were always squelchy and staticky. At least fifty times a day we would hear someone say, "Do you read me?" or "I can't read you." Then one or the other would drive a half mile to another vantage point and try it again. It could be a challenge to get the message across.

. . . everyone who hears these words of mine and puts them into practice . . .

In these closing words of the greatest sermon ever preached, Jesus is effectively asking us, "Do you read me?" *Do you read me* means more than just, "Can you hear me now?" It means not only, "Do you hear me?" but also, "Do you understand what I am saying?" To be sure, there is a way of reading that bypasses hearing. Similarly, there is a way of hearing that bypasses listening. It is why Jesus is ever saying things like, "Whoever has ears to hear let them hear."

. . . everyone who hears these words of mine and puts them into practice . . .

To hear in the way Jesus wants us to hear means to listen beyond mere comprehension. It means to press one's comprehension into contemplation and yet it can't stop there. Our reading, which is to say our deep hearing, must lead us from comprehension to contemplation and on to consecration—which is the offering up of our broken and incomplete selves in exchange for the wholeness and fullness of Jesus. It is how the Word becomes flesh in us.

This is what it means to read the Word of God in the power of the Spirit of God. We must learn to read in the way of Jesus, which is to say we must learn to read with Jesus in the power of the Spirit. It does not come naturally to us. It only comes supernaturally.

That's where we miss it. We think better must mean more. Our natural reflex is to think we need to read more of the Bible more of the time. What if that's wrong? We need to learn to read it better, which means from a supernatural perspective. What if it actually means reading fewer verses with more depth over longer periods of time? What if it actually does begin with listening and hearing rather than reading and studying? What if it looks more like the one-year chapter rather than the one-year Bible?

Do you read me?

Read this next sentence aloud, so your ears can hear it: "The grass withers and the flowers fall, but the word of our God endures forever" (Isa. 40:8).

Faith, after all, does not come by reading, but by hearing.

The Prayer

Yes, Lord, we want to read you in a deeper way than ever before in our lives. We confess, our reading has been shallow and often superficial. We impose our own meanings and categories and we have a way of sifting out what challenges us deepest. Would you train us to read you, Jesus, and in reading the Word of God to learn to read you more deeply into and out of it. Grant us the gift of forgetting so much of what we think we already know that we may learn anew and afresh—this time from you. We pray in your name, Jesus, amen.

The Questions

- Do you ever read the Word of God aloud? If not, why not? Have you ever considered that the Word of God was written not to be read but to be heard? After all, for much of the history of the world, most people could not read. The printing press only came around about five hundred years ago. There's something about hearing. Will you try this practice more often? Do you read me?

Have You Found God's Word for the Year?

4

MATTHEW 7:24–27 | "Therefore everyone who hears these words of mine and puts them into practice is like a wise man who built his house on the rock. The rain came down, the streams rose, and the winds blew and beat against that house; yet it did not fall, because it had its foundation on the rock. But everyone who hears these words of mine and does not put them into practice is like a foolish man who built his house on sand. The rain came down, the streams rose, and the winds blew and beat against that house, and it fell with a great crash."

Consider This

In recent years a new kind of practice is cycling through the church around the new calendar year. It is the practice of coming up with a word you want to focus on for the new year. People come up with a word like "intentional" or "new" or "grace" or "encourage" and the list goes on. Many will cite a verse of Scripture as the originating idea behind their word. I suppose it is okay, as far as trends go, but in my years of seeing this at work, it usually only goes until about March at best or until the next popular Bible reading app springs up.

It turns out to be a nice spiritual New Year's Resolution-ishy kind of sentimental intention. It holds about as much power as human words tend to have, which is none. And, frankly, I have never heard anyone choose a word like "suffering" or "martyr" or "death" for their word for the year. People tend toward the squishy, happy, good-feels kinds of abstractions that in time become meaningless.

So why am I so curmudgeonly about such a practice? Isn't it a good thing for Christians to at least be making some semblance of an effort to be focused at the start of a new year? No. It's not. Friends, in case you haven't noticed, the house is on fire and it is time to stop congratulating each other for bringing our water guns.

I don't want to know your word for you. I want to know God's Word for you. *Your* word is meaningless. Even if it is based on God's Word, it is still meaningless because it is a reduction of the real thing. When I ask you for God's Word for you, I want to hear a constellation of words, formed into a sentence or two or even a paragraph—with punctuation and inflection and a precisely revealed sequencing of concepts, images, and ideas. Why?

"The grass withers and the flowers fall, but the word of our God endures forever" (Isa. 40:8).

I was talking to one of my bandmates the other day when he mentioned his grandson's word for the year. He's a freshman in college at Clemson, I believe. It blew me away. His word: 1 Corinthians! Yes! The whole sixteen chapters! Come on, church! Let's not be reducing ourselves to one distilled word of our own imagining. Let's expand it out to as many of God's words as we can begin to wrap our souls around every single day for the next 365-day journey around the sun.

Let's take a longer view—say ten years. In ten years if you have ten single words they will mean little to nothing. If you have ten words from the Word of God, verses, or texts—and these texts have been engraved on your heart—you will have inestimable treasure that will never stop generating interest and dividends and returns on returns on returns. It starts afresh this year. So what is God's Word for you?

"The grass withers and the flowers fall, but the word of our God endures forever" (Isa. 40:8).

The Prayer

Yes, Lord, we are weary of our words because our words do not endure. We want more of your words, which endure forever. Would you lead us to a verse, a passage, a text—one we could immerse ourselves in? We want for your Word to be written on our hearts. So we offer you our good aspirations and receive from you your deeper intentions. Open your Word to us and let the same Holy Spirit who breathed it into being breathe it into my deepest mind and heart. We pray in Jesus' name, amen.

The Questions

- So how about it? Do you have a word from God? Not a theme word or a catchphrase but a bona fide word from the Word of God?

5 What Is Your First Word Every Day? How about Your Last Word?

PSALM 19:7–9 | The law of the Lord is perfect,
refreshing the soul.
The statutes of the Lord are trustworthy,
making wise the simple.
The precepts of the Lord are right,
giving joy to the heart.
The commands of the Lord are radiant,
giving light to the eyes.
The fear of the Lord is pure,
enduring forever.
The decrees of the Lord are firm,
and all of them are righteous.

Consider This

So how about it? What is your first word of the day? What is your last word?

I'll go first. Too many times, my first word of the day comes from an e-mail or a text message. Somehow I just have this need to read what someone else has said to me while I slept. Last word? Too many times, my last word comes from Netflix. I watch some episode of a show until I drift off to sleep.

So, the two most critical places for the influence of my life are being given to a) someone else's agenda for me (i.e., messages) and b) meaningless entertainment. I first became convicted about this a couple of years back. It hit me one day—why do I not give God the first and last words of my day? From that moment onward, with ups and downs and varying degrees of success and failure, I have done it. So why does this matter?

"The grass withers and the flowers fall, but the word of our God endures forever" (Isa. 40:8).

Would you like for your soul to be refreshed? Would you like to become wise? Would you like your heart to be filled with joy? Would you like to see things with the radiance of insight? Would you like to be possessed of the purity of God? Would you like to be formed in true righteousness?

So all of these are the fruits of the gift of God's Word. God's Word does not work like a magical incantation. He works through miraculous infusion. That's where the First Word—Last Word work comes into play. Remember, faith comes by hearing. Transformation comes by transfusion. The Word of God must get into our lives in a comprehensive and even totalizing way.

So, picking up where we left off yesterday, what is the word (verse, text, passage) from God's Word for you? If you don't have one, then start with Isaiah 40:8.

Whatever it is, this is going to be your first word every morning and your last word every night. The practice is simple. Upon waking, speak that word aloud. Before bed, speak that word aloud. Rinse. Repeat.

For your soul it will have the effect of putting $100 in a high-interest yielding bank account every single day. It is the literal loading of your soul with revival, wisdom, joy, radiance, light, purity, solidity, righteousness, and we could go on. And faith—it's not believing what I am saying is true. It is actually doing it. First Word. Last Word. God's Word.

The Prayer
Yes, Lord, we thank you for your Word, which endures forever. We want to feed our souls the food of forever, every day, multiple times a day, beginning with the first word and the last word. We want our ears to hear your Word, because faith comes by hearing. And we want our soul to receive your Word by the power of your Spirit—through miraculous infusion. This is our hearts' desire. In Jesus' name, amen.

The Question
- Will you take the First Word—Last Word—God's Word challenge?

6 My First Word—Last Word—God's Word

PSALM 130 | Out of the depths I cry to you, Lord;
   Lord, hear my voice.
Let your ears be attentive
   to my cry for mercy.

If you, Lord, kept a record of sins,
   Lord, who could stand?
But with you there is forgiveness,
   so that we can, with reverence, serve you.

I wait for the Lord, my whole being waits,
   and in his word I put my hope.
I wait for the Lord
   more than watchmen wait for the morning,
   more than watchmen wait for the morning.

Israel, put your hope in the Lord,
   for with the Lord is unfailing love
   and with him is full redemption.
He himself will redeem Israel
   from all their sins.

Consider This

My First Word—Last Word—God's Word Text is Psalm 130. It will take me weeks to rememberize* the whole psalm, but verse 5 has already become the money pitch so far.

I wait for the Lord, my whole being waits, and in his word I put my hope.

I listened to the whole psalm on my Bible app before sleep last night. Early in the morning, in that hushed and (coming to be) sacred time between waking and rising, I begin to think

---

* *Rememberize*, for new readers, means the slow loading of the long-term memory, as opposed to memorize, which means the fast loading of the short-term memory. Google "Learning to Rememberize the Word of God" for more.

on this word. Then I reminded myself to say it aloud, which I do. Hearing it leads me to ruminate on it.

I wait for the LORD, my whole being waits, and in his word I put my hope.

As I rolled it around in my awakening mind, it hit me. *I wait for the Lord*, yes; *my whole being waits*, yes; *and in his Word I put my hope* . . . well . . . yes . . . and . . . no.

If I'm honest, and you know I try to be, I am hoping more in what I want the Lord to do for and in my life. In other words, I am hoping he will fix the brokenness in me and all the broken things in my life. That's what I'm hoping for. Is that wrong? No. It's just not right. And there it was, in the predawn silence of the morning, as this first word broke the sound barrier and shed light across the synapses of my soul—*and in* his word *I put my hope.*

Psalm 130 cut its first groove—and a deep impression at that—into my heart.

. . . and in his word *I put my hope.*

I am not waiting on the Lord and trusting in some outcome. I am waiting on the Lord and while I am waiting, I am putting my hope in his Word. Waiting can be passive, but putting my hope in his Word—now's there's something to do with my *whole being* that is active, movement even.

I wait for the LORD, my whole being waits, and in his word I put my hope.

The Prayer

Yes, Lord, we wait for you. We can't say with our whole beings just yet, but we are going to get there. And maybe that's what you are waiting for in us—for our whole beings to get there to the waiting place on you. In the meantime, we are going to focus on rooting our hope in your Word. It will be our first word and it will be our last word and something tells us you are going to make it a whole lot of other words in between. We pray in Jesus' name, amen.

The Question
- Will you choose a text from Scripture and make it your first word of every day and your last word of every day? That's the challenge. Let's go!

Moving from the Extraction Approach to the Immersion Approach

7

PSALM 130 | Out of the depths I cry to you, Lord;
   Lord, hear my voice.
Let your ears be attentive
   to my cry for mercy.

If you, Lord, kept a record of sins,
   Lord, who could stand?
But with you there is forgiveness,
   so that we can, with reverence, serve you.

I wait for the Lord, my whole being waits,
   and in his word I put my hope.

> I wait for the Lord
> > more than watchmen wait for the morning,
> > more than watchmen wait for the morning.
>
> Israel, put your hope in the Lord,
> > for with the Lord is unfailing love
> > and with him is full redemption.
> He himself will redeem Israel
> > from all their sins.

Consider This

This little psalm is itself its own massive cathedral of revelation. They all are. I have heard it before, though I am almost certain I have never heard anyone preach or teach on it. Like so many other texts in the Bible I've read it a number of times before and been impressed, but invariably moved on. My tendency with biblical texts and most everything else, is to read it, try to extract some meaning from it, and move on. After reading it a few times or studying it a little, I am pretty sure I've gotten what there is to get there. Next!

In other words, I have an extraction approach. The Word of God requires an immersion approach. Flip the script. It's not what can I get out of these words, but how can I get into this word and the world of this word. The question is not, as most of us have been trained to ask, "How is this relevant?" The operative inquiry of the immersion approach is, "What is being revealed here?" And every text of Scripture is a well of inexhaustible revelation.

Psalm 130 invites me into a world of revelation. It takes me out of my flat and fixed world and into a cathedral space of vast dimensions. There is so much in here to see. My attention has been drawn first to verse 5.

I wait for the LORD, my whole being waits, and in his word I put my hope.

My whole being waits. I wake up every morning to find myself waiting on the Lord. Or do I? It will not take long into the day until my "whole being" is running in ten different directions and not waiting at all. In fact, nothing in me wants to wait.

I need the Word of God to have authority in and over my life. There's something about me speaking the word aloud that somehow makes it so. When I give God's Word the priority and prominence, it unleashes his Word as a living, active, and "movemental" word in my life. It always accomplishes the purposes for which he sends it. *My whole being waits.* It has me asking myself, *Am I cultivating the inner wherewithal to bring my whole being into submission to God?* This doesn't just happen in my life. It happens as I move to the second part of the verse, which I am already doing by speaking it aloud: *and in his word I put my hope.*

In this everyday, somewhat simple way, the Word of God is sorting and sifting my whole being—gathering up my disparate parts of my fragmented self, putting me back together, bit by bit, morning by morning, night by night, until my whole being is wholly waiting upon him.

The Prayer

Yes, Lord, we thank you for your Word. Thank you for waking us up with your Word. Thank you for putting us to bed with your Word. Thank you for the endless gift of your eternal Word. Forgive us for our flippant approach to your Word. Forgive us for thinking we already get it, just because we've read it once or twice. Forgive us for our self-centered way of reading. Train us in this way of immersion into your Word and the world of your Word. May your Word remake our world as we learn to wait on you with our whole beings. In Jesus' name, amen.

The Questions

- What do you make of this contrast I am drawing between an extraction approach to God's Word and an immersion approach? How would you say what I am trying to say?

8 Carpool Catechesis

PSALM 18:1–2 | I love you, O Lord, my strength.
The Lord is my rock, my fortress and my deliverer;
  my God is my rock in whom I take refuge,
  my shield and the horn of my salvation, my stronghold.

Consider This

You've heard of carpool karaoke, the practice made famous by late-night talk host James Corden. How about carpool catechesis? It's something I stumbled onto as a young parent. As our kids aged out of bedtime routines and rituals, we had to find new ways to try and sow the Word of God into their lives. In other words, at what other points in their lives did I have them as a captive audience? It became the car ride to school.

Every day on the way to school I would try to lead them in saying the Apostles' Creed, praying the Lord's Prayer, and antiphonally reciting the Beatitudes and the Twenty-Third Psalm—or at least one of these things depending on the day and who had put off studying for their test until the car ride to school. Anyhow, the last thing I would say to them as they exited the car was the first line of Psalm 18. I would say, "I love you, O Lord," and they would say, "my strength." Then I would tell them that I loved them by name. (As they got older I had to abbreviate the last part by saying "LML"—short for Love my Lily—to which they would reply, "LMD"—short for Love my Dad; on the off chance that one of their friends might hear these verbal exchanges as the doors opened and closed on the mini-van!) I digress.

As I write, my youngest, Sam, is about to get his driver's license, which will bring this long season of carpool catechesis to an end. I'm happy-sad about this. In so many ways I have come up short as a parent. My children are not paragons of the Christian faith. I wish I had more time. As I reflect back, it occurs to me that I am not confident in my parenting at all. I am confident in the Word of God and I know this Word has been sown into their lives in ways that largely participated with their willingness—even if at times only passively. Time will tell.

Here's one regret. I wish I had gotten to verse 2 of Psalm 18:

The L<small>ORD</small> is my rock, my fortress and my deliverer; my God is my rock in whom I take refuge. He is my shield and the horn of my salvation, my stronghold.

Look at the sheer layering going on here. Count them—seven brilliant, visceral images stacked upon each other like stones, crafting the very imagery he speaks of as he speaks it. In fact, David is singing these words out to God and the world: ROCK—FORTRESS—DELIVERER—REFUGE—SHIELD—SALVATION—STRONGHOLD.

Even more impressive to me is his use of another term. He uses it eight times: *my*.

The Prayer

Yes, we love you, O Lord, our strength. You are our rock, our fortress and our deliverer; you are our rock in whom we take refuge. You are our shield and the horn of our salvation, our stronghold. Jesus, we want this "my" to become stronger and more real in this year ahead. Holy Spirit, would you lead us into all of these places in ways more real than ever before. We pray in Jesus' name, amen.

The Question

- How might you immerse in this word from Psalm 18?

Morning, Coffee, and the Word of God

9

PSALM 143:8–10 | Let the morning bring me word of your unfailing love,
  for I have put my trust in you.
Show me the way I should go,
  for to you I entrust my life.
Rescue me from my enemies, Lord,
  for I hide myself in you.
Teach me to do your will,
  for you are my God;
may your good Spirit
  lead me on level ground.

Consider This

There's something about the morning and the Word of God.

I come from a farming family. From an early age, I remember my father's morning chair and side table which always held a sizable Bible with a brown leather cover. He was often long gone to the farm before we even woke up. I don't remember why, but around my sixth- or seventh-grade year I began to wake up early. I discovered my dad sitting in his chair, coffee cup in hand, with the big brown Bible open on his lap. One of those mornings I motioned for Dad to slide his Bible across the floor to me. Soon, my mom got me a Bible just like his. There began, for me, the intersection of three of the greatest things in life: morning, coffee, and the Word of God.

There are so many references to the morning in the Word of God. Today's text provides a good example: *Let the morning bring me word of your unfailing love, for I have put my trust in you. Show me the way I should go, for to you I entrust my life.*

In Psalm 108, David speaks of "awakening the dawn." The prophet Isaiah offers this word: "The Sovereign Lord has given me a well-instructed tongue, to know the word that sustains the weary. He wakens me morning by morning, wakens my ear to listen like one being instructed" (50:4).

Hear Jeremiah's famous word on the morning: "Because of the Lord's great love we are not consumed, for his compassions never fail. They are new every morning; great is your faithfulness" (Lam. 3:22–23).

Then there's the morning practice of our Lord, the Word made Flesh: "Very early in the morning, while it was still dark, Jesus got up, left the house and went off to a solitary place, where he prayed" (Mark 1:35).

The celebrated twentieth-century Chinese church leader Watchman Nee famously referred to the early mornings as "The Morning Watch." The psalmist captures it in Psalm 130:6: "I wait for the Lord more than watchmen wait for the morning, more than watchmen wait for the morning."

There's something about the morning and the Word of God. And coffee!

The Prayer

Yes, Lord, thank you for the morning. There's something about waiting for you and waiting for the morning as we read your Word. Would you awaken us morning by morning and give us an instructed tongue, that we might be refreshed for the day and have words to refresh the weary. Holy Spirit, lead us to consecrate the mornings afresh to you. We pray in Jesus' name, amen.

The Questions
- How are the mornings for you? Delight? Drudgery? What if the Word of God could turn you into a morning person?

God's Way: Perfect. God's Word: Flawless. 10

PSALM 18:30–36 | As for God, his way is perfect:
    The Lord's word is flawless;
    he shields all who take refuge in him.
For who is God besides the Lord?
    And who is the Rock except our God?
It is God who arms me with strength
    and keeps my way secure.
He makes my feet like the feet of a deer;
    he causes me to stand on the heights.
He trains my hands for battle;

> my arms can bend a bow of bronze.
> You make your saving help my shield,
>   and your right hand sustains me;
>   your help has made me great.
> You provide a broad path for my feet,
>   so that my ankles do not give way.

Consider This

The Word of God is utterly incredible because it reveals the truth about a God who is actually and absolutely true. God's way: perfect. God's Word: flawless. Psalm 18 is an absolute marvel.

Recall how David built a mighty fortress with words which described the Mighty Fortress who is God: MY ROCK. MY FORTRESS. MY DELIVERER. MY REFUGE. MY SHIELD. MY SALVATION. MY STRONGHOLD (see Ps. 18:2).

This was not theoretical for David. Psalm 18 is not a happy-clappy song. David knew enormous trouble and experienced life-shattering struggles and, as a consequence, like so many of us, he knew debilitating despair. Take a look at verses 3 through 5.

> I called to the Lord, who is worthy of praise,
>   and I have been saved from my enemies.
> The cords of death entangled me;
>   the torrents of destruction overwhelmed me.
> The cords of the grave coiled around me;
>   the snares of death confronted me.

Many, many people today are entangled in the cords of death. Certainly you know them and may be one of them. Many are overwhelmed this very day with the torrents of destruction. I sometimes marvel at the people who turn away from God in disbelief because of the presence of suffering and evil in the world. "To whom will you turn?" I want to ask them. Everyone faces such storms in life. No one escapes trial, trouble, and tragedy. No one is immune from the suffering brought on by this broken and corrupted world. And as sure as we get through one difficulty, another brews on the far horizon. In the face of this, what we must have is more confidence in the Word of God and the God of the Word.

Look how David, a very real, flawed, failed, faith-filled human being walked out his confidence in God. Will you savor these words with me today, reading them aloud so your ears can hear them?

> As for God, his way is perfect:
>   The Lord's word is flawless;
>   he shields all who take refuge in him.
> For who is God besides the Lord?
>   And who is the Rock except our God?
> It is God who arms me with strength
>   and keeps my way secure.
> He makes my feet like the feet of a deer;
>   he causes me to stand on the heights.
> He trains my hands for battle;
>   my arms can bend a bow of bronze.

> You make your saving help my shield,
>   and your right hand sustains me;
>   your help has made me great.
> You provide a broad path for my feet,
>   so that my ankles do not give way.

The Word of God is utterly incredible. I want to add a second word and a third word and a fourth word. I think, what if I had a word for every hour? There still would not be enough hours, would there?

The Prayer

Yes, Lord, your ways are perfect. Your Word is flawless. You are our rock, our fortress, our deliverer, our refuge, our shield, our salvation, our stronghold. Though many times we do not understand why things happen as they do, we are learning to trust in you. We are learning that though you did not will them or want them or cause them, you are powerfully at work through them for our good, for others' gain, and for your glory. In the face of the greatest insecurity, you arm us with strength and make our way secure. Lord Jesus, you are our way. You are our truth. You are our life. We trust in you. For your namesake we pray, amen.

The Questions

- Do you find yourself wanting to add yet another text and another to the queue of first words and last words? But what could be better, right?

Shower Words

11

JOHN 15:1–3 | "I am the true vine, and my Father is the gardener. He cuts off every branch in me that bears no fruit, while every branch that does bear fruit he prunes so that it will be even more fruitful. You are already clean because of the word I have spoken to you."

Consider This

You are already clean because of the word I have spoken to you.

Have you ever considered that the Word of God cleanses us? What if we don't have to clean ourselves up? What if, as the old hymn has it, "He speaks; and listening to his voice, / new life the dead receive. / The mournful broken hearts rejoice, / the humble poor believe."*

What if that's really true?

You are already clean because of the word I have spoken to you.

It would mean his Word does the work. It would mean our main task is simply listening to him. Think back with me to Transfiguration Mountain. Remember after all the celestial light show was over, the voice of God thundered from heaven: "This is my Son, whom I love. Listen to him!" (Mark 9:7).

---

* Charles Wesley, "O for A Thousand Tongues to Sing," 1739, Public domain.

What if we don't have to do all the work? In fact, what if we don't have to do any of the work? What if our work is that of showing up, bowing down, listening to him, and truly receiving his Word—which is also to receive him. What if Jesus does all the work?

There's a text near the end of Ephesians 5, where Paul begins by talking about marriage. He makes an analogy to Christ and the church. Then he gets so carried away with Jesus he almost forgets he was talking about marriage in the first place. I want us to hear that word about Jesus, in just this sense, without the nuptial analogy: "Christ loved the church and gave himself up for her to make her holy, cleansing her by the washing with water through the word, and to present her to himself as a radiant church, without stain or wrinkle or any other blemish, but holy and blameless" (Eph. 5:25b–27).

Jesus loved us.

Jesus gave himself up for us.

Jesus makes us holy.

Jesus cleanses us by the washing with water through the word.

Jesus presents us to himself as radiant, without stain, or wrinkle, or any other blemish.

Jesus presents us to himself as holy and blameless.

What if it's true?

You are already clean because of the word I have spoken to you.

If we can receive and believe this revelation, it will change everything . . . without us having to change everything ourselves.

You see this notion that we have to do all (or any) of the work. There is a biblical term for that. It's called *slavery*. This notion that Jesus has already done all the work and he's looking for someone humble enough to audaciously receive it and walk on it like water. There's a biblical term for that too. It's called *freedom*.

I like to speak this word aloud every morning when I am in the shower. As the water washes over my body, this word of Jesus rings out through my voice and into my ears where it flows straight into my soul and deepest self—like a holy, cleansing flood of freedom.

You are already clean because of the word I have spoken to you.

The Prayer

Yes, Lord, we are already clean because of the word you have spoken to us. What a relief. We are not clean because we tried harder to be better or we focused more on not sinning. We are clean because of the word you have spoken to us. Bring deep awakening to our faith to this end, to believe your word, to trust in it, to walk out onto the waves of it and find myself jubilantly alive in the freedom of your Spirit. Yes, Lord, we are already clean because you have cleansed us and no other reason. We pray in Jesus' name, amen.

The Questions
- Why is it so hard for us to simply receive? Why do we so desperately need to feel like we are adding something to the mix, whatever it may be? Why is it so hard for us to bring absolutely nothing to the party but our naked, broken, and being-healed soul?

12 On the Source and Other Sources

PSALM 119:9–16 | How can a young person stay on the path of purity?

> By living according to your word.
>
> I seek you with all my heart;
>
> > do not let me stray from your commands.
>
> I have hidden your word in my heart
>
> > that I might not sin against you.
>
> Praise be to you, Lord;
>
> > teach me your decrees.
>
> With my lips I recount
>
> > all the laws that come from your mouth.
>
> I rejoice in following your statutes
>
> > as one rejoices in great riches.
>
> I meditate on your precepts
>
> > and consider your ways.

I delight in your decrees;
I will not neglect your word.

Consider This

As I grow in faith, I find myself learning more and more obvious things I overlooked before. For instance, in the earlier part of my journey I thought I needed to read lots and lots of books about God, faith, discipleship, and the Bible. I became enamored with many sources. Certainly these sources have been helpful and yet I wonder if they were the best use of my limited time. As I move further down the path, I am more and more enamored with and fixated on one source—the Word of God.

Another shortcoming of much of my reading history has been to begin with the wrong question. Upon reading a text I want to immediately ask, "What does this mean?" The question of meaning is important, but this often leads me away from the text to other sources and other voices in order to try to interpret the text. This is not bad. It is just out of sequence.

I am learning to ask a more basic question, "What does it say?" And I ask this question not only first, but second, and third. In order to get at what a text says, I need to read it and read it again and maybe a hundred more times for a hundred more days. Then I need to let my reading lead to hearing and to ruminating and meditating and to rememberizing. Note how the psalmist describes this approach in this magisterial Psalm 119.

Notice the diversity of engagement in the moves from "I seek you with all my heart" to "I have hidden your word in my heart" to "With my lips I recount all the laws that come from your mouth" to "I meditate on your precepts and consider your ways" to "I delight in your decrees; I will not neglect your word."

"The grass withers and the flowers fall, but the word of our God endures forever" (Isa. 40:8).

The Prayer

Yes, Lord, thank you for your Word and for your eternal patience with us. Bring us into the heart, mind, and spirit of the psalmist, who loves you and so loves your Word. Slow us down to listen and hear your Word, to ponder what it says before pressing it for some deeper meaning. Train me to see the obvious, to recognize the surplus right on the surface. Keep me in step with your Spirit as I immerse myself in your Word. I pray in Jesus' name, amen.

The Questions

- Has your impulse been to jump into studying God's Word even before allowing the Word to speak to you on its own terms? Do you tend toward reading more devotional literature or more of the straight source document of the Word of God?

The Word Is Not Magic, but It Is Miraculous

13

MATTHEW 4:1–4 | Then Jesus was led by the Spirit into the wilderness to be tempted by the devil. After fasting forty days and forty nights, he was hungry. The tempter came to him and said, "If you are the Son of God, tell these stones to become bread."

Jesus answered, "It is written: 'Man shall not live on bread alone, but on every word that comes from the mouth of God.'"

Consider This

The Word of God is not magical, but it is miraculous.

Theoretically, magical words, or a spell, work in a mechanistic fashion. If we get the words or the spell right, the magic happens. This is not how the Word of God works.

It brings temptation #1 in the wilderness into an interesting focus. After his baptism, Jesus was sent into the wilderness by the Holy Spirit where for forty days he fasted and was tempted by Satan.

Satan actually tempts Jesus to use the Word of God as magic. "Tell these stones to become bread," he says. He, in essence, invites Jesus to "name it and claim it." He wants him to use words like magic.

Reading the Bible better means we must understand the larger context of this story and encounter. We are meant to understand this scene and setting as a revisiting of the wilderness in the story of Exodus. As Israel came through her baptism through the parting of the Red Sea and their deliverance from Egypt, so Jesus came through his baptism in the Jordan River. Because Israel did not believe God's promise, they wandered forty years in the wilderness. Jesus spent forty days, one for each year of Israel's wandering, in the wilderness. God provided manna (a form of bread) for the Israelites every single day of the forty years. He did not do it by magic, though, turning stones into bread. He did it by his powerful and miraculous Word. Stones to bread would have been a spectacle. They would have wanted to learn to trick. What words do I say to get this to happen? The miracle happened by the divine Word alone. Note how Jesus responded to the temptation:

Jesus answered, "It is written: 'Man shall not live on bread alone, but on every word that comes from the mouth of God.'"

The point of the bread was not the bread but the one who provided the bread and to understand that the real bread was the very Word from his mouth. It makes it all the more stunning when later we will hear Jesus, the Son of God, declare, "I am the bread of life" (John 6:35).

Jesus is the Word of God perfectly revealed as incarnate in the person of God. Jesus is the place where the Word of God and person of God are revealed in perfect union. They exist in a perfect union of convergence and correspondence.

In other words, the Word of God is not some kind of magically microwaved happy meal. It is part and parcel of God himself—miraculous.

How does this apply to our lives? We marvel at it. We behold. We bow down. We feast on these words.

"Man shall not live on bread alone, but on every word that comes from the mouth of God."

But remember, this is not bread you can make or make happen. It is the bread of heaven.

There is no recipe—only revelation.

This is the real Wonder Bread.

The Prayer

Yes, Lord, it is truly a marvel that you both give the bread of your Word and you *are* the Word who is the bread of life itself. We can only bow in awe at the mystery of you. Take us deeper into the mystery of who you are. We want to know your Word like food. This means we want to hunger for you. Holy Spirit, make it so. We pray in Jesus' name, amen.

The Questions

- Are you growing in your appreciation for the nature of the Word of God? Are you seeing the connection between the Word of God as written in the Bible and the Word of God as revealed in the person of Jesus Christ?

14 The Simple and Comprehensive Invitation of the Word of God

DEUTERONOMY 6:4–9 | Hear, O Israel: The Lord our God, the Lord is one. Love the Lord your God with all your heart and with all your soul and with all your strength. These commandments that I give you today are to be on your hearts. Impress them on your children. Talk about them when you sit at home and when you walk along the road, when you lie down and when you get up. Tie them as symbols on your hands and bind them on your foreheads. Write them on the doorframes of your houses and on your gates.

Consider This

It is interesting how the very next words after the central words in all of Scripture (a.k.a. the Shema—vv. 4–5) are these: "And these words that I command you today shall be on your heart" (v. 6 ESV).

Simple translation: To love God is to love his Word.

I marvel at the way so many believers think and approach the love of God as a matter of feeling and affection. I feel some manner of affection for God, therefore I love God. It's not bad, just thin and quite superficial. I marvel at how so many supposed committed Christians have very little touch with God's Word. They believe it. They salute it. But when it comes to any significant engagement with God's Word, it is just not there. They tend to read the thoughts of others about God's Word, even mine, and yet they have very little significant engagement with the source of God's Word.

By significant engagement with God's Word I do not mean Bible study. To be sure, Bible study is good, but what I am talking about is far simpler on the one hand and far more comprehensive on the other.

Simple: "And these words that I command you today shall be on your heart" (v. 6 ESV).

Comprehensive:

Impress them on your children.

Talk about them

- when you sit at home,
- when you walk along the road,
- when you lie down,
- when you get up.

Tie them as symbols on your hands.

Bind them on your foreheads.

Write them on the door frames of your houses.

Write them on your gates.

The Word of God will be impressed on our hearts only to the extent it shows up in our everyday, walking-around lives. I think we would all agree with the simple aspiration. The challenge comes with the comprehensive expression. If we are not pressing the simple aspiration into a comprehensive expression we are fooling ourselves about the Word of God being anything more than a naive sentimental reality in our lives.

One more thing. We are not yet talking about implementing or practicing the Word of God in our lives. We must begin with the simple and comprehensive exposure and expression of the Word of God itself—sitting, walking, lying down, getting up, children, hands, foreheads, door frames, gates . . . Why? Remember: "The grass withers and the flowers fall, but the word of our God endures forever" (Isa. 40:8).

The Prayer

Yes, Lord, we want to impress your Word on our hearts. Forgive us for leaving it at that level; the wanting-to level. We want to make this practical, tangible, and real. Would you show us practically how we might get the Word of God out of the Bible and make it present and visible in our everyday lives? This seems challenging and even strange in ways. We need leadership, but more than that, we probably just need nerve. We pray in Jesus' name, amen.

The Question

- How have you found ways to do these kinds of things with the Word of God in your everyday life?

Enlarging Our Vision of the Word of God

15

DEUTERONOMY 6:4–9 | Hear, O Israel: The Lord our God, the Lord is one. Love the Lord your God with all your heart and with all your soul and with all your strength. These commandments that I give you today are to be on your hearts. Impress them on your children. Talk about them when you sit at home and when you walk along the road, when you lie down and when you get up. Tie them as symbols on your hands and bind them on your foreheads. Write them on the doorframes of your houses and on your gates.

Consider This

For the Word of God to gain real prominence in our lives, at least two things must happen. First, we must gain a much larger perspective on Scripture and consequently a much grander vision. Second, we must learn to read at a whole new level.

In pursuit of the fulfillment of Deuteronomy 6:4–9, I began collecting the words from Scripture that themselves testify about Scripture. In other words, what does the Bible say about itself? A couple years back I began to craft these words from Scripture about itself into a kind of short creedal affirmation. Here at the midway point of the series I wanted to share it as an encouragement. I encourage you to affirm it aloud.

I believe in the living Word of God, who is the Son of God, Jesus Christ.

And I believe in the written Word of God, the Bible, the Holy Spirit–inspired authority of the people of God.

God's Word endures forever,

is sweeter than honey,

more precious than gold,

sharper than a double-edged sword,

judging the thoughts and attitudes of the heart.

This Word is perfect, trustworthy, right, radiant, pure, firm, and flawless.

It refreshes the soul,

makes wise the simple,

gives joy to the heart,

is a lamp to my feet and a light to my path.

God's Word teaches, corrects, rebukes, and trains.

It cleanses and prunes, feeds and nourishes, is purposeful and powerful.

It burns like a fire in my bones.

It always accomplishes the purposes for which it is sent.

God's Word will be on my heart, on my gate, on my doorpost.

I will talk about it when I lie down and when I wake up and when I walk along the road.

I will read, ruminate, rememberize, research, and rehearse it, building my life on the rock of God's Word.

Indeed, "the grass withers and the flowers fall, but the word of our God endures forever."

It will be the first Word. It will be the last Word. This is God's Word.

I wonder if you would consider affirming this each morning for the rest of our series?

The Prayer
Yes, Lord, there is no other word that endures forever. We want to stake our lives on the promises of God, which is your Word. Would you enhance our perspective, enlarge our vision, and open our lives wide that your Spirit might write your Word on our hearts? We pray in Jesus' name, amen.

The Question
- How might this affirmation become part of your faith formation?

Learning to Anchor in the Word of God
16

PSALM 84:1–2 | How lovely is your dwelling place,
   Lord Almighty!
My soul yearns, even faints,
   for the courts of the Lord;
my heart and my flesh cry out
   for the living God.

Consider This

On the previous entry, I noted that if we are to grow in our love for the Word of God and find it deeply impressed on our hearts, two things must happen: 1) a greater vision of the Word of God and 2) a deeper, simpler, and more comprehensive way of reading.

Over the past several years I have been practicing ways of reading the Bible for all it's worth with all I've got. I am finding it to be quite different than what most others are doing. Most people I encounter go in one of two directions. One group reads devotional materials. Their engagement of Scripture consists of whatever the particular devotional material might reference. I am not eschewing this approach. It is fine, as far as it goes, however, it just doesn't go deep enough to adequately anchor a person in the Word of God.

The other direction people tend to take is that of reading plans. They are trying to cover large swaths of Scripture each day in their devotional time. From a ninety-day reading plan to a one-year plan or even a two-year plan, they are trying to get through the whole Bible. I don't want to eschew this approach either. It, too, is fine as far as it goes, however, it just doesn't go deep enough to adequately anchor a person in the Word of God.

I am a massive advocate for a deep familiarity with the scope and sweep of the story of Scripture. I am also a strong proponent of reading devotional material. We can learn and grow a lot by reading others' writings concerning Scripture.

And while I don't consider the Daily Text "devotional material" in the usual use of the term, it is a form of devotional commentary on Scripture.

The practice I am trying to pioneer is something altogether different. I am going to call it "anchoring." Anchoring means living with a particular text, usually a passage with some length or heft, for a significant period of time. It consists of daily engagement with what I call the 5 Rs of anchoring: Reading. Ruminating. Rememberizing. Researching. Rehearsing. I will focus on those in the coming days, but anchoring is the process of engaging a text of Scripture in a simple yet comprehensive fashion to the end that we have laid claim to the text for the rest of our lives and the text has laid claim to us.

As an example, I have been reading Psalm 84 for the past nine months, almost every single day. Many days I have simply read the text aloud from my Bible, focusing on hearing it well. Many other days I turned on my Bible app and let it read the text to me while I again focused on listening.

Read Psalm 84 aloud. Focus on hearing it. I will be referring to it throughout the rest of the book.

> How lovely is your dwelling place,
>   Lord Almighty!
> My soul yearns, even faints,
>   for the courts of the Lord;
> my heart and my flesh cry out
>   for the living God.
> Even the sparrow has found a home,

and the swallow a nest for herself,
where she may have her young—
a place near your altar,
Lord Almighty, my King and my God.
Blessed are those who dwell in your house;
they are ever praising you.

Blessed are those whose strength is in you,
whose hearts are set on pilgrimage.
As they pass through the Valley of Baka,
they make it a place of springs;
the autumn rains also cover it with pools.
They go from strength to strength,
till each appears before God in Zion.

Hear my prayer, Lord God Almighty;
listen to me, God of Jacob.
Look on our shield, O God;
look with favor on your anointed one.

Better is one day in your courts
than a thousand elsewhere;
I would rather be a doorkeeper in the house of my God
than dwell in the tents of the wicked.
For the Lord God is a sun and shield;
the Lord bestows favor and honor;
no good thing does he withhold
from those whose walk is blameless.

Lord Almighty,
blessed is the one who trusts in you.

The Prayer

Yes, Lord, we want to learn to anchor ourselves in your Word so that your Word might anchor itself in us. Train us in this way of patient reading that slows down and covers less ground. We have the image of a drilling or mining operation. What greater treasure could we claim than your Word. Holy Spirit, would you orient us with this way of anchoring ourselves in the Word of God to the end that the Word become flesh in us. We pray in the name of Jesus, who is this way in perfection. Amen.

The Questions

- Is there a passage of Scripture you are led to anchor into in the coming season? Would you like to explore this? Is there someone you could share in this practice with—perhaps even over the same text—an anchor buddy?

Anchor Buddies 17

COLOSSIANS 3:16 ESV | Let the word of Christ dwell in you richly, teaching and admonishing one another in all wisdom, singing psalms and hymns and spiritual songs, with thankfulness in your hearts to God.

Consider This

Let's take a further step into the practice we are calling anchoring. Anchoring means living with a particular text, usually a passage with some length or heft, for a significant period of time in a simple yet comprehensive fashion—to the end that we have permanently laid claim to the text and the text has permanently laid claim to us.

Anchoring is a way of deep reading. Today's text gets at the big idea.

Let the word of Christ dwell in you richly, teaching and admonishing one another in all wisdom, singing psalms and hymns and spiritual songs, with thankfulness in your hearts to God.

Something that does not readily occur to many of us (especially us rugged individualist Americans) is the "you" in the New Testament is almost always second person plural. The Southern translation would be "all y'all." The Word of God is written to us personally but not individually. It is actually written to us in the context of our relatedness. The original hearers of the New Testament would have heard it as written to "us" first and "me" second. This must become increasingly so for us—you and me. This has tremendous implications for the way we read the Bible. Even when we read alone and by ourselves, we are reading together in community.

To let the Word of Christ, which is the Word of God, dwell in us richly—this is anchoring. So how does this shift from *me* to *we*? This is where the concept of an anchor buddy comes into play. An anchor buddy is a person with whom you share an anchor text. About fifteen years ago, my friend and fellow Seedbed FarmTeam member Mark Benjamin and I were on a long car ride and we started reading Psalm 19. We began to speak it back and forth, phrase by phrase, one to another. It became a quest to learn the text and as we grew in it, it became a deep means of encouraging one another. To this day, when we are together, one of us will kick it off, "The heavens declare the glory of God," and the other will say, "The skies proclaim the work of his hands," and we are off to the races. The Word has become a kind of bond between us. In this way, the Word dwells in us richly. As we process our way through the text, the Word is teaching us and admonishing us in all wisdom. We are anchor buddies.

You have heard me tell of the Carpool Catechesis with my kids. Within that practice, my son Sam and I have become anchor buddies around Psalms 23 and 24 and the Beatitudes, speaking them back and forth and back and forth until we have laid claim to the texts and the texts to us and then some more. This summer I made another anchor buddy around Psalm 84. Each morning, we would text the whole psalm back and forth, verse by verse, and, sometimes, phrase by phrase until we had it. This Word became like the cement of our newfound friendship.

It doesn't have to be a long text either. One longtime friend and mentor of mine and I have exchanged Psalm 146:8. One of us will say, "The Lord lifts up," and he will respond, "those who bow down." There is no better, higher, and more enduring word we can speak to one another than the Word of God.

The Prayer

Yes, Lord, we want to learn to anchor ourselves in your Word that your Word might anchor itself in us. Lead us to others with whom we can read deeply, with whom we can anchor in the Word together. Thank you for those anchor buddies in our lives. Holy Spirit, would you open up the existing relationships in our lives to this way of reading together—our spouses, our children, our parents, our bands, friends from church, neighbors, and beyond. We pray in the name of Jesus, who has anchored himself to us eternally. Amen.

The Questions
- Do you have an anchor buddy? Ever had one? Would you like to move in this way of the Word with others? Who might be such a person in your life?

18 Keeping Our Eye on the Ball of the Word of God

COLOSSIANS 1:15–20 | **The Son is the image of the invisible God, the firstborn over all creation. For in him all things were created: things in heaven and on earth, visible and invisible, whether thrones or powers or rulers or authorities; all things have been created through him and for him. He is before all things, and in him all things hold together. And he is the head of the body, the church; he is the beginning and the firstborn**

from among the dead, so that in everything he might have the supremacy. For God was pleased to have all his fullness dwell in him, and through him to reconcile to himself all things, whether things on earth or things in heaven, by making peace through his blood, shed on the cross.

Consider This

Anchor buddies, let's try this one!

ME: Wake up, sleeper, and rise from the dead . . .

YOU: And Christ will shine on you!

By the way, that is Ephesians 5:14 in case you were not aware. I learned with my teenaged children that my wake-up call has little effect. So I am switching over to Ephesians 5:14 as my wake-up call, because the Word of God has power and it never returns void. Whether they get out of bed or not, they will have heard the Word of God. After all, it doesn't say, "Wake up, sleeper, and get out of bed." We actually have a much larger problem than that. It says, "rise from the dead." The most beautiful part of the text, however, is the word *shine*. For my money, it is a bit of a benign English word to use for the Greek term *epiphauskó* (pronounced ep-ee-fow'-o). You will recognize the related word *epiphany*.

Ep-ee-fow'-o means something like "reveal." Epiphany happens when we finally really see what we have been looking at. This is why we "fix our eyes on Jesus," "the Word made flesh" because he is himself the source of never-ending eternal epiphany, the revealed one who never stops revealing "the Way and the Truth and the Life," the shining one whose very nature it is to shine. I love how Paul puts it to the Christians at Colossae—especially how The Message renders it:

> We look at this Son and see the God who cannot be seen. We look at this Son and see God's original purpose in everything created. For everything, absolutely everything, above and below, visible and invisible, rank after rank after rank of angels—*everything* got started in him and finds its purpose in him. He was there before any of it came into existence and holds it all together right up to this moment. (Col. 1:15–17)

And all of this focus on the Word of God—it is not so we can be better Bible students or know more about the Bible. It is that we might know Jesus Messiah as Savior, Lord, Teacher, Friend, and on we could go. If we want to see the perfect expression, explication, and exposition of the Word of God as Scripture we look to Jesus Messiah, the Word of God as second person of the Trinity. Not only do we see the whole counsel of God made manifest in Jesus, he is the one who will instruct and teach us the whole counsel of God as revealed in Scripture.

But let's keep our eye on the ball, remembering the point of it all—growing in relational abiding union with Jesus himself—who brings us into the embrace of the Father and fills us to overflowing with the Holy Spirit. It is important to grasp the nuance of what we are saying here. Anchoring is not anchoring in a book per se. And it is certainly not amassing more knowledge about the Bible or even *about* God. It is anchoring in the Word who is Jesus who inspired the Word which is Scripture and who reveals himself through the Scriptures and Spirit that we might know him beyond knowledge and that we might be filled to the measure of all the fullness of God. And all of this so we, by the grace of God, might become the spitting image of Jesus in and through the distinctive life, personhood, and personality he has given to us.

Again, anchor buddies, "Wake up, sleeper, and rise from the dead . . ."

And you say . . . this time with feeling . . .

The Prayer

Yes, Lord, you are the image of the invisible God—the Word made flesh. We want this Word to be made flesh in us, in our everyday, walking-around lives. This will depend on you shining on us and in us and through us. And we know for this to happen, we need to stay awake and yet we can't even stay awake apart from you. We want to know you more, Jesus. Teach us the Scriptures as you reveal yourself in and through them to us. This is such a mystery and yet you are putting handles on it that we might hold on. We pray in your name, Jesus, amen.

The Questions

- Are you grasping this clear, simple, and yet nuanced relationship between the Word made flesh as Jesus and the Word as revealed through Holy Scripture? How would you articulate it in your own words?

J. D. WALT

19 How God's Word Designs the World It Declares

PSALM 1:1–3 | Blessed is the one
   who does not walk in step with the wicked
or stand in the way that sinners take
   or sit in the company of mockers,
but whose delight is in the law of the Lord,
   and who meditates on his law day and night.
That person is like a tree planted by streams of water,
   which yields its fruit in season
and whose leaf does not wither—
   whatever they do prospers.

Consider This

Anchor buddies! Let's try this one today:

ME: I wait for the Lord, my whole being waits . . .

YOU: And in his Word I put my hope.

By the way, that is Psalm 130:5, my First Word–Last Word text for the year. I am learning to speak it aloud upon waking, in the quiet stillness, before I get out of bed. Once I say it aloud, I find the words begin to plow through the field of my mind. Scripture often comes to us in the first instance as a prescriptive text. In other words, it is prescribing some way of thinking or intentioning or acting. But the more I engage with a text, the more it becomes descriptive—creating the very reality of which it speaks.

As an example, I will read and say, "I wait for the Lord, my whole being waits, and in his Word I put my hope," and I will think, *Yes, that is what I need to do. I need to wait on the Lord and to hope in his Word. Of course! I need to be more patient.* It becomes something I should try harder to focus around and work on. *But when will I do that*, I wonder. It is so easy for it to remain as a kind of prescription, which I carry as a good intention. But when I begin to dwell on the text—the biblical word is *meditate*—turning the words over in my mind, allowing them to roam freely through my heart and soul, I find myself actually experiencing what it says.

I discover as I ruminate on the words, "I wait for the Lord, my whole being waits," I find myself waiting on the Lord and focusing on gathering up all the parts of myself and bringing them into some integrated sense of my whole being. My mind, heart, soul, physical body, strength, feelings, passions, all of it, comes into the waiting room. The text begins to describe the very thing that is happening. Yes, I am waiting for the Lord, my whole being is waiting. And as I find myself in the waiting place, I am in fact, hoping in his Word.

"I wait for the Lord, my whole being waits, and in his word I put my hope" (Ps. 130:5).

As long as I focus on this text as something I need to do, I am not doing it. When I dwell on the word itself, it begins to create the reality. Psalm 84 offers another great example of this dynamic of prescriptive versus descriptive at work: "My soul yearns, even faints, for the courts of the Lord; my heart and my flesh cry out for the living God" (v. 2).

This text tells the deepest truth of every human being who has ever walked the face of the earth. Blessed are the ones who come into an aligned agreement with it. Just saying it doesn't make it so. It takes anchoring down into the text, laying claim to it, and allowing it to lay claim to you. To say that God's Word does not return to him void is to say God's Word designs the world it declares. To engage the Word of God in this fashion is to be shaped by the Word.

This is a deep thought today. Do you read me?

Again, anchor buddies,

ME: I wait for the Lord, my whole being waits . . .

YOU: And in his Word I put my hope.

The Prayer

Yes, Lord, we are weary of our own best intentions. They are so seductive and yet so superficial. We don't want to be shaped by our best intentions, but rather by the Word of God's powerful action. We want to come into deep-hearted alignment and clear-minded affirmation of your Word. Help us understand the working of your Word and how our working needs to give way to waiting on you. Holy Spirit, interpret this way of the Word to us. We pray in Jesus' name, amen.

The Question

- Are you ready to trade your own prescriptive initiative of what you think you ought and should be doing and doing more to structure and strengthen your faith—which is a heavy burden—for the easy yoke of allowing the substance of the Word of God to shape your life? This can be a very hard concept to grasp. Stay with it.

17:17 My New Double Domino

20

JOHN 17:17 | "Sanctify them by the truth; your word is truth."

Consider This

I love double domino Scripture texts. I discovered another one today . . . John 17:17.

Sanctify them by the truth; your word is truth.

I'm not into numerology or secret Bible codes by any stretch, and the chapter and verse numbers are not part of the inspired text. It still feels like a holy serendipity to me, kind of like a bingo, when a text like this lands in the double domino zone.

Sanctify them by the truth;

your word is truth.

I love how Jesus makes the truth synonymous with God's Word. They are one in the same.

If God sanctifies us by the truth and his Word is truth, then God sanctifies us by his Word. So what does it mean to sanctify or to be sanctified? It means to be made holy. But what does that mean? To be made holy means to be consecrated.

But what does that mean? To be consecrated means to be set apart as a vessel for divine purposes. That which is sanctified is prepared to be anointed and filled with the Holy Spirit. The Word sanctifies. The Spirit fills.

It doesn't stop there. It can't stop. That's the problem with a lot of teaching about holiness. Because *holy* literally means "set apart," it gets translated to mean to live apart from any possible contaminating people or influences. It becomes a caricature of biblical holiness and people come up with absurd phrases like, "holier than thou." Holiness gets equated with being super religious. And who wants that! Holiness actually means super-related; super-relatable to God, oneself, and others. The Word sanctifies. The Spirit fills. And the Son sends. "As you sent me into the world, I have sent them into the world" (v. 18).

Sanctified. Spirit-filled. Sent.

Rinse. Repeat.

It begins with sanctified.

Sanctify them by the truth; your word is truth.

It makes sense then that we would want to be utterly saturated by this super relatable Word . . . when we lie down, when we wake up, when we walk along the road, with our children, with our friends, written on our gates, our doorposts, on our foreheads, on our hands, and in every way impressed on our hearts.

Sanctified. Spirit-filled. Sent.

Rinse. Repeat.

That's Double Domino 17|17.

The Prayer

Yes, Lord, sanctify us, sanctify us by the truth. Your Word is truth. We want to be sanctified by your Word. We are weary of trying to sanctify ourselves by our own best intentions and dedicated efforts. Show us that the way is as simple as being saturated by your Word. You are the sanctifier. You are the Spirit-filler. You are the sender. We are humble participants. At least that's what we want to become. Make it so. We pray in Jesus' name, amen.

The Questions

- What is your notion of holiness? Have you had a caricatured idea of it? Do you want to be holy—in the way of Jesus? What would that look like? What if it became about beholding instead of behaving? What if we are actually made holy by being in contact with the Holy One and his Holy Word?

Turn On Your Lights! 21

PSALM 119:105 ESV | Your word is a lamp to my feet and a light to my path.

Consider This

It happened again the other night. I'm sure you have had the same experience. I was driving down a busy, largely unlit boulevard and I saw a car up ahead driving with their lights off. Per usual, they were completely unaware. I noticed people coming from the opposite direction were flashing their lights. I began to click between high and low beam from the rear. I then began to flash my headlights on and off. I saw a car up ahead start to pull out into the lane of oncoming traffic only to slam their breaks at the last minute upon finally spotting the darkened car. I zoomed up alongside the car, wildly waving my arms, and finally getting their attention to turn on their headlights.

A vehicle without lights is a hazard to its occupants as well as everyone else on the road around them.

Your word is a lamp to my feet and a light to my path.

We readily think of this text as it relates to our seeing the path ahead of us. When our path is lit by the Word of God, it also illuminates the path for others around us as well. Imagine, though, a town or city where most of the vehicles did not have headlights. It would be treacherous getting around after dark, wouldn't it? Unfortunately, it is an apt metaphor for the state of affairs in this country if not much of the world today. People are without the Light. More and more people are driving around with their lights off. It's why we must have awakening.

Your word is a lamp to my feet and a light to my path.

Think about the distinction in the text. On the one hand, the Word of God shines the light around my feet so I can avoid tripping over obstacles or unlevel ground. That is kind of like the low beam headlights. On the other hand, the Word of God shines light on the path ahead, showing us where we are headed. That is kind of like the high beam headlights. That is the Word of God, illuminating what is right in front of us and what is out ahead of us.

Here's the challenge. The Word of God is not the Bible on our shelf or even the one in our hand. The Word of God, on the everyday paths of life, consists of the Scripture that has been impressed on our hearts, embedded in our minds, and enfleshed in our real lives.

Some newer cars these days have a setting where they will automatically shift between high and low beam based on the path ahead. That is what a person steeped and saturated in the Word of God is like. It becomes automatic. Wisdom and counsel and guidance seem to flow into and out of them almost effortlessly. They know things others do not know because the Word has given them insight. They hear things others do not hear because the Word has given them attunement. They see things others do not see because the Word has given them illumination.

Remember the double domino text from yesterday: "Sanctify them by the truth; your word is truth" (John 17:17). The Word of God, from constant exposure, makes us luminous. Our path is not lit from a book in our hand as though it were a flashlight. It is lit by the Word unleashed in our lives.

One more reason we say: Wake up, sleeper, and rise from the dead . . .

And you say . . . (Hint: see Eph. 5:14)

The Prayer

Yes, Lord, your Word is a lamp to our feet and a light to our path. We want to walk in the Light as you are in the Light. Your Word is our guidance, our wisdom, and our luminosity. By your Spirit, your Word is becoming our character and our constitution. We love your Word, Lord, and in loving your Word, we are loving you. Thank you, Jesus. We pray in your name, amen.

The Questions

- How are you letting the Light of the Word shine into your heart, mind, soul, and strength? How are you engaging the source of the Light, the Word of God?

22 Learning Scripture like Language

ISAIAH 50:4 | The Sovereign LORD has given me a well-instructed tongue,
    to know the word that sustains the weary.
He wakens me morning by morning,
    wakens my ear to listen like one being instructed.

Consider This

A Daily Text reader e-mailed me their First Word—Last Word text: Isaiah 50:4. It reminded me of a scene in the 2005 movie *Walk the Line*. Did you see the movie? It tells the origin story of Johnny and June Carter Cash. There's a scene early in the movie where John and his older brother Jack are in in their beds talking before going to sleep. Jack is reading his Bible. John asks him something like, "Jack, why are you always reading that Bible?" to which Jack replies, "How can I help anybody if I don't know the right story to tell them?" You are seeing the connection, too, aren't you?

The Sovereign Lord has given me a well-instructed tongue, to know the word that sustains the weary. He wakens me morning by morning, wakens my ear to listen like one being instructed.

One of my regrets in life is I never learned a foreign language. Over the years, though, I have come to understand Scripture as a kind of language. In one sense, it is a foreign language, yet in a much deeper way, Scripture is our most native language. The best way to learn language is by the simple and comprehensive way of immersion. We must immerse ourselves in the world of the Word. That's the whole point of this series. We are largely taught to read the Bible for its practical relevance to our lives. This causes us to read it from an extraction point of view, which keeps us asking, "What can I get out of it?" That is not wrong. It is just woefully inadequate. It is the equivalent of going to another country and constantly asking, "How do you say . . . where is the bathroom?" and "How much does it cost?"—just the super-relevant, functional, and practical essentials.

An immersion approach requires a submission to the language itself and the humility of realizing just how much instruction we need and how deep it must go. It is about having that getting-up word (first word), that lying-down word (last word), anchor-buddy word, walking-along-the-road word, talking-with-our-children word, written-on-our-gate, doorpost, forehead, hand, impressed-on-our-heart, enfleshed-in-our-lives word.

Ultimately, we aren't trying to learn to speak in "Bible-ease" but to inhabit the language of love. Scripture gives us the grammar, the syntax, the vocabulary, the frameworks, idioms, metaphors, the lexicons that can be translated into every culture and for the sake of every people group, indeed—for every single person. Isn't that what today's text is getting at?

The Sovereign LORD has given me a well-instructed tongue, to know the word that sustains the weary. He wakens me morning by morning, wakens my ear to listen like one being instructed.

The fascinating thing about language is how it is so vastly interconnected and interwoven, producing what we might call a stunningly coherent complexity. The earlier referenced reader's e-mail came in response to Psalm 119:105: "Your word is a lamp to my feet and a light to my path."

Here's what he wrote: "In an offbeat way this (Ps. 119:105) connects with my first Word/last Word verse Isaiah 50:4. Check it out if you find the time."

The Holy Spirit made a cross-referential connection between these texts for this reader—in an "offbeat way" he noted. That's how learning Scripture a language works. That's how immersion in revelation works. Extraction for relevance has its place, I suppose—if you want to be a tourist. The people of God, however, are not tourists. We are on pilgrimage. We are pilgrims, journey-women and men and children. We are marching to Zion. Let's give the great hymn writer, Brother Isaac Watts, the last word today.

> Come, ye that love the Lord,
> And let your joys be known;
> Join in a song with sweet accord,
> Join in a song with sweet accord,
> And thus surround the throne,
> And thus surround the throne.
> We're marching to Zion,
> Beautiful, beautiful, Zion:
> We're marching upward to Zion,
> The beautiful city of God.[*]

The Prayer

Yes, Lord, we are marching to Zion and not only are we learning to speak a language, you are teaching us to sing it. It is the melody of divine love. So would you wake us up each morning to listen as those being instructed? Holy Spirit, immerse us in the Word of God such that not only are we refreshed but we become your refreshment for others. I want to be immersed in the wonder of the world your Word is making. We pray in your name, amen.

---

[*] Isaac Watts, "Marching to Zion," 1683, Public domain.

The Questions
- Are you grasping the difference between the extraction approach to reading Scripture and the immersion approach? How does this analogy of language and learning language help? What connections are you making?

23 The Wonderful Way of Immersion in the Word of God

PROVERBS 2:1–8 | My son, if you accept my words
  and store up my commands within you,
turning your ear to wisdom
  and applying your heart to understanding—
indeed, if you call out for insight
  and cry aloud for understanding,
and if you look for it as for silver
  and search for it as for hidden treasure,
then you will understand the fear of the Lord
  and find the knowledge of God.
For the Lord gives wisdom;
  from his mouth come knowledge and understanding.
He holds success in store for the upright,
  he is a shield to those whose walk is blameless,
for he guards the course of the just
  and protects the way of his faithful ones.

Consider This

Proverbs 2 gives us a powerful vision of what immersion in the Word of God looks like. Notice the eight levels of engagement prescribed here:

1. Accept my words.
2. Store up my commands within you.
3. Turn your ear to wisdom.
4. Apply your heart to understanding.
5. Call out for insight.
6. Cry aloud for understanding.
7. Look for it as for silver.
8. Search for it as for hidden treasure.

Read the list again; this time slowly. This is not an urgent appeal for strenuous activity. It is a beckoning invitation to deep immersion.

There is also a decisive set of outcomes:

1. You will understand the fear of the Lord.
2. You will find the knowledge of God.
3. You will receive wisdom.
4. You will enjoy success.
5. Your walk will be shielded.
6. Your course will be guarded.
7. Your way will be protected.
8. You will understand what is right, just, and fair.
9. You will know every good path.
10. Wisdom will enter your heart.
11. Knowledge will be pleasant to your soul.
12. Discretion will protect you.

13. Understanding will guard you.
14. Wisdom will save you from the ways of wicked men.
15. Wisdom will save you from adultery.
16. You will walk in the ways of the good.
17. You will keep to the paths of the righteous.
18. You will live and remain in the land.

Enough said.

The Prayer

Yes, Lord, thank you for your Word, without which we would be utterly lost. Would you bring us into the simple and comprehensive way of immersion in your Word? We want to accept, store up, turn our ears, apply our hearts, call out for insight, cry aloud, and search for hidden treasure. Holy Spirit, illuminate us by the Word of God. In Jesus' name, amen.

The Question

- How are you growing in your practices of immersing yourself in Scripture?

24 Formed by the Word, Filled by the Spirit

JEREMIAH 18:1–6 | This is the word that came to Jeremiah from the Lord: "Go down to the potter's house, and there I will give you my message." So I went down to the potter's house, and I saw him working at the wheel. But the pot he was shaping from the clay was marred in his hands; so the potter formed it into another pot, shaping it as seemed best to him.

Then the word of the Lord came to me. He said, "Can I not do with you, Israel, as this potter does?" declares the Lord. "Like clay in the hand of the potter, so are you in my hand, Israel."

Consider This

Sometimes I can get so immersed into what I'm thinking about, talking about, teaching, or doing that I can lose perspective on the big picture. That's when I run into a text like Jeremiah 18:1–6. We have been focusing so much of late on being immersed in the well of the Word of God. I thought it might be good to send up a drone camera that could give us a bird's-eye view of what is happening as a result of our practices of immersion. Aristotle said the soul never thinks without a picture, which I think he must have learned from Jeremiah. Jeremiah gives us a marvelous picture in this word from God about the potter's wheel.

This is the word that came to Jeremiah from the Lord: "Go down to the potter's house, and there I will give you my message." So I went down to the potter's house, and I saw him working at the wheel. But the pot he was shaping from the clay was marred in his hands; so the potter formed it into another pot, shaping it as seemed best to him.

We are being shaped—formed—by the Word in order that we might be filled by the Spirit.

We are the clay. The Word of God in the hands of Jesus by the Living Water who is the Holy Spirit forms and shapes us into holy vessels able to hold, display, and convey the presence of God. I think the most important insight from the text is that the clay does not shape itself. The clay does not tell the potter what to make of it.

I was talking to Taylor Gindlesberger (who serves on the Seedbed Farm Team), who is also our resident potter. As a seminary-trained student of Scripture, she commented how most people neglect the real context of the text, noting how Jeremiah was warning of the immanent destruction of Israel if they did not repent. She then said an interesting thing about the nature of clay. She talked about how she has a large bucket filled with scraps of clay that for whatever reason didn't work out the first time on the wheel. She noted how those scraps get dried out and the reason she puts them in the bucket is so she can fill it with water to recondition the clay to be reshaped on the wheel later. The experience of the immersion of the clay in the water effectively makes it like new again. It reminded me of the rest of today's text:

Then the word of the Lord came to me. He said, "Can I not do with you, Israel, as this potter does?" declares the Lord. "Like clay in the hand of the potter, so are you in my hand, Israel.

Taylor spoke of how this encourages her faith—that she is not in charge of working to get her life shaped right. She said she is learning to rest like the clay immersed in the Word and Spirit and becoming responsive to the initiative of Jesus rather than needing to bring the initiative herself. And then she said the most brilliant thing of all: "I am learning how God pulls together all the broken pieces of all our lives and refashions us into a beautiful vessel we could have never even imagined."

The Prayer

Yes, Lord, you are the potter and we are the clay. Thank you for the way you form us by your Word, shape us by your Spirit that we might be filled with your very splendor. Thank you for the way you pick up the broken pieces, immerse them in the water of your Word and Spirit, and bring them forward for yet more shaping and crafting. We don't want to resist your work. We want to trust our lives into your hands—completely. You made us. Only you can remake us. We trust you, Jesus. Amen.

The Questions

- How do you understand the ways in which you are being shaped and formed by the Word of God these days? Are you learning the lesson that you are not the potter—that Jesus is? Are you learning to be more responsive and less restless and determined by your own initiative and activity? It's a hard lesson to learn. Sometimes it takes a season in the bucket with the scraps.

J. D. WALT

25 Trading Our Assumptions for God's Assurances

1 SAMUEL 3:1–7 | The boy Samuel ministered before the Lord under Eli. In those days the word of the Lord was rare; there were not many visions.

One night Eli, whose eyes were becoming so weak that he could barely see, was lying down in his usual place. The lamp of God had not yet gone out, and Samuel was lying down in the house of the Lord, where the ark of God was. Then the Lord called Samuel.

Samuel answered, "Here I am." And he ran to Eli and said, "Here I am; you called me."

But Eli said, "I did not call; go back and lie down." So he went and lay down.

Again the Lord called, "Samuel!" And Samuel got up and went to Eli and said, "Here I am; you called me."

"My son," Eli said, "I did not call; go back and lie down."

Now Samuel did not yet know the Lord: The word of the Lord had not yet been revealed to him.

Consider This

People often ask me, "How on earth do you come up with something new for the Daily Text every single day?" My answer is, "I don't." Seriously, I don't come up with anything. I ask Jesus to give me something. I ask him to reveal himself and his Word to me. Then I wait. And I trust what comes. It comes not in the form of an idea I come up with. It comes in the form of sensing the gravitational pull of one or another of his words. Today it was 1 Samuel 3:7.

Now Samuel did not yet know the Lord: The word of the Lord had not yet been revealed to him.

Two simple and super-related questions today:

1. Do you know the Lord?
2. Has the Word of the Lord been revealed to you?

Here's what's interesting to me about this text.

The boy Samuel ministered before the Lord under Eli. . . . Samuel was lying down in the house of the Lord, where the ark of God was.

Samuel was surrounded by the things of God and yet he did not know God.

He slept in the house of the Lord, in the very room which held the ark of the covenant. Samuel was in the very presence of God but did not know it. He knew about God, but he did not know God. In other words, he was asleep to the very reality in which he lived.

This is the big problem with slumber. You don't know it when you are sleeping. You don't know you were asleep until you wake up. It's often the question of a person who wakes up after being in deep sleep, "How long was I asleep?"

In other words, I don't know what I don't know. Here's how I put it: the greatest impediment to my own awakening is the fact that I'm pretty sure I am already awake. I remind myself that Jesus knows me completely, yet I know him in part and the part of him I don't know is far greater than the part I do know. I want to know him fully, even as I am fully known. So I humble myself and I tell him this. And I realize that the further I go in building my knowledge about God and surrounding myself with the things of God can actually deceive me into thinking I have already arrived.

And though I have written thousands of Daily Text entries by now, every day I begin at the beginning again; lining up at the starting line, waiting on the Lord and the revelation of his Word, pressing in to know him more, humbling myself in his presence, and by pure grace, waking up a bit more to his more-ness, his fullness, and his more than enough-ness. And here's what I find. As I lay my self-assured assumptions on the altar, he meets me there with Holy Spirit–inspired assurances.

This is what I call the awakened life.

The Prayer

Yes, Lord, we want to know you more. We want to trade our assumptions for your assurances. We humble ourselves before you and confess there is so much more of you to know than we presently know. And yet the more we know you the more we want to know you more and to know more of you. Jesus, the more we know you the more we love you and the more we love others. Open the eyes of our hearts to this ongoing and ever deepening way of awakening. Awaken us to the moreness, the fullness, the more-than-enoughness of who you are. We pray in Jesus' name, amen.

The Questions
- Do you know the Lord? Has the Word of the Lord been revealed to you? Are you living off of your own assumptions or are you receiving assurances?

Calling for a Verdict 26

DEUTERONOMY 32:45–47 | **When Moses finished reciting all these words to all Israel, he said to them, "Take to heart all the words I have solemnly declared to you this day, so that you may command your children to obey carefully all the words of this law. They are not just idle words for you—they are your life. By them you will live long in the land you are crossing the Jordan to possess."**

Consider This
"They are not just idle words for you—they are your life."

As we near the end of this season of First Word—Last Word—God's Word, and the case is about to go to the proverbial jury (a.k.a. you all), I find myself wondering if I have said enough. Has the case been made? Did I leave anything out?

That's exactly what's going on in today's text. We find ourselves at the end of Israel's forty-year wandering in the wilderness. They are on the eve of entering the promised land. Moses has called all his witnesses. He recounted the full story of God's faithfulness. He articulated the blessings for obedience and the curses for disobedience. He rehearsed the full covenant of the Law with the whole nation. He brought it all down to the most compelling call for a verdict ever recorded. Check it out:

> This day I call the heavens and the earth as witnesses against you that I have set before you life and death, blessings and curses. Now choose life, so that you and your children may live and that you may love the Lord your God, listen to his voice, and hold fast to him. For the Lord is your life, and he will give you many years in the land he swore to give to your fathers, Abraham, Isaac and Jacob. (Deut. 30:19–20)

And if this were not enough, he wrote a song and led the people in singing it. (Now there's an idea for us!) After all that, we get today's text.

"Take to heart all the words I have solemnly declared to you this day. . . .

They are not just idle words for you—they are your life."

Permit me a few brief observations.

1. The Word of God is not an idle word. It is powerful and movemental. We turn the Word of God into an idle word in our life to the extent we leave it bound in a book.
2. The antidote is to "Take to heart all the words . . . and solemnly declare them to ourselves and each other."
3. The Word of God is not *for* my life. It *is* my life. See the difference?

"Now choose life, so that you and your children may live and that you may love the Lord your God, listen to his voice, and hold fast to him. For the Lord is your life . . ."

Have you reached a verdict?

The Prayer

Yes, Lord, we want to choose life. Over and over and over again we want to choose life and yet it comes back to choosing life in this moment. You, Lord Jesus, are our life. Your Word is our life. We love you, Lord. We listen to your voice. We hold fast to you. And we want this for our children and their children and their children. Holy Spirit, make it so. In Jesus' name, amen.

The Questions

- How is the Word of God becoming loosed from the bindings of the book and unleashed in your everyday life? Are you learning to solemnly declare it? How is it moving from being *for* your life to *being* your very life?

27 How I Got My House Back

PSALM 19:11-13 | By them your servant is warned;
in keeping them there is great reward.
But who can discern their own errors?
Forgive my hidden faults.
Keep your servant also from willful sins;
may they not rule over me.
Then I will be blameless,
innocent of great transgression.

Consider This

"They are not just idle words for you—they are your life" (Deut. 32:47).

Back in the fall I had an epiphany—you know, the sudden and surprising realization of an often-obvious kind of thing that somehow you never quite realized before. I realized that I lived in a dog house. Lucy, our little twelve-pound Satan of a dog we rescued from hell (a.k.a. the pound) is a Jack Russell Terrier/Chihuahua—two dogs who should have never been left alone in the same backyard. Anyway, back in the fall, it hit me one day that Lucy didn't live in our house. We lived in her house. I won't go into all the gory details, but one of Lucy's main features is she seems to shed her entire coat of hair twice per day. It's insane, and horrible, and no matter how many times I sweep, there's more.

Anyway, this epiphany led me into a type of grace-filled repentance (as epiphanies are apt to do). I would no longer enslave myself to the broom and all the futility of sweeping, which is really just a dog hair relocation tactic. (Kind of like trying to manage your sin instead of letting Jesus eradicate it.) So what did repentance look like in this situation? I acquired a knock-off Roomba. A Roomba is one of those little circular robot-like devices that moves around your house on its own schedule and initiative and vacuums up anything in its path. Somehow, it manages to cover the entire room over time in the most seemingly random way possible. It just does it. And, oh my! It can eat its weight in dog hair multiple times a day.

I know you are wondering, *Why are you telling me this? What on earth does this have to do with the Word of God?* Here's why. When we loose the Word of God from its book-ish bindings and unleash it in our lives, it works like a Roomba. All you have to do is keep it charged and emptied out of all it collects. It is not an idle word. It is an active, moving, productive, powerful, transformative, healing, comforting, working Word.

As we anchor ourselves in the Word every single day through reading, ruminating, rememberizing, researching, and rehearsing; as we make it our first word and our last word; as we immerse ourselves in this Word, which is our life, the Word just works. This is how it becomes a lamp to our feet and a light to our path, living and active, probing and piercing, helping and healing. This is how it becomes like bread for the eater and seed for the sower. This is how Jesus makes the simple wise, gives joy to the heart, and gives light to the eyes. This is how he orders our steps, directs our path, warns us of danger, alerts us to temptation, cleans us up, and prunes us back. As we impress the Word on our hearts, talk about it along the way, write it on our gates and our doorpost, bind it to our wrist, text it to our friends, anchor in with our families, the Word does the work. Don't hear me wrong. Our part is not passive. It's just not primary. Our work is to simply work with the Word. The Word made flesh through the Word revealed in text by the power of the Spirit actually does the work.

It's kind of like that Roomba—the day I got it was the day I got my house back. Lucy now lives in a human house again. And I'm looking into making dog hair down pillows. Anybody interested?

"They are not just idle words for you—they are your life" (Deut. 32:47).

The Prayer

Yes, Lord, we want your Word, which is to say who you are and what you have revealed, to be loosed and unleashed in our lives, running all the time, in the foreground, in the background, actively, passively, and in every other way. Forgive us for the way we have allowed it to be idle in our lives by not engaging it fully through our lives. Holy Spirit, inspire, illumine, and ignite our lives by your Word. In Jesus' name, amen.

The Questions
- How does the Roomba story help you? What connections are you making? How are you reclaiming your proverbial house?

When the Word of God Asks Us a Question (Question 1 of 3)

GENESIS 3:8–9 | Then the man and his wife heard the sound of the LORD God as he was walking in the garden in the cool of the day, and they hid from the LORD God among the trees of the garden. But the LORD God called to the man, "Where are you?"

Consider This

The Word of God is filled with stories, statements, commands, exclamations, declarations, even declamations, and yet it is also laden with questions. I am not talking about our questions concerning God or God's Word. I am talking about God's questions to people, and by extension to us. It is worth a series all to itself. God asks questions.

One of the most piercing questions God asks in the Bible is the very first question God asks. We see it in today's text. The question comes after Adam and Eve turned away from the command of God to eat from every tree in the garden save one. In the wake of their rebellion, they tried to hide from God. Then God asks this question.

"Where are you?"

The whole notion of God asking a question raises an even larger question, doesn't it? God is omniscient. God knows everything, which implies the answer to any and every question. The notion that God even has a question is a towering absurdity—unless God is not asking the question for his own sake. What if God asks us questions for our sake? What if God asks us precisely the kinds of questions we wouldn't tend to ask of ourselves? Questions like . . .

"Where are you?"

It's interesting how Adam responds to the question with some information but not an answer. It is not an easy question to answer. I think I know the answer until I try to answer it. So where am I?

There's a greeting practiced in Sub-Saharan Africa where upon meeting one person will say, "Sawa bona," which means, "I see you." The other will respond by saying, "Sik hona," which means, "I am here." When God says, "Where are you," it's not because he doesn't know. It's like he wants us to know that he knows. It's as though God were saying, "I see you. Even though you feel lost and alone. Even though you may be trying to hide. Even though you may not even be able to tell me exactly where you are, I want you to know, 'I see you.'" I believe he's looking for a response something like, "I am here," and to say that in as much detail as we can muster. It's not that we are telling God something he doesn't know; we are coming home to ourselves in God's presence. It's why in our banding work, the first question we ask is, "How is it with your soul?" It's what we call the "locating" question.

So where are you? Remember, it's not where should you be or where do you wish you were. It's, "Where are you?" I'll go first.

I am here. As I write this, I'm in Franklin, Tennessee, on the recovering side of a painful and tragic family collapse. I am a bit lost and walking through what I believe to be the outskirts of what has been a long wilderness season. I am alone, often lonely, and yet filled with faith, hope, and love. I am following Jesus of Nazareth, the Messiah—Lord of heaven and earth, with no back-up plan, bail-out scenario, and nowhere else to go. I am searching for church and coming up short in finding her. I am seeking the kingdom with more success. I am in a flourishing and yet life-support dependence on the Word of God and the Spirit of God. I am in the process of trading in the search for the happiness this world has to offer in exchange for the quest after the inextinguishable joy of the Lord—come what may. I am strangely content, yet in need, and yet want for nothing. I have traded in wants in exchange for the deeper longings. It is well with my soul.

The Prayer

Yes, Lord, thank you for the questions you ask in your Word, when you know the answer all along. Thank you for this question, "Where are you?" Thank you for the way you help us to be honest, vulnerable, and transparent before you and others, bringing us home to ourselves. Thank you for seeing us and loving us and being so patient with us. Teach us how to be this way in relationship with ourselves and with others. In Jesus' name, amen.

The Question
- Okay, your turn. *"Where are you?"*

29 When the Word of God Asks Us a Question (Question 2 of 3)

1 KINGS 19:9 | **And the word of the Lord came to him: "What are you doing here, Elijah?"**

Consider This
Elijah, the prophet of God, is in a world of hurt. He has just come from the famous Battle of the Gods on Mt. Carmel. He finds himself in the wilderness state we might call Vertigo, both running from God while running to God. He has lost his sense of direction, balance, and will to go on.

He traveled from Mt. Carmel to Mt. Horeb (a.k.a. "the Mountain of God") and he went into a cave—which brings us to our text:

And the word of the Lord came to him: "What are you doing here, Elijah?"

Like Adam, Elijah responds to God's question with a lot of information without answering the question:

> He replied, "I have been very zealous for the LORD God Almighty. The Israelites have rejected your covenant, torn down your altars, and put your prophets to death with the sword. I am the only one left, and now they are trying to kill me too." (1 Kings 19:10)

So God decides to peel back a layer of the onion that is the cosmos and take Elijah into what we might call the thin place: "The LORD said, 'Go out and stand on the mountain in the presence of the LORD, for the LORD is about to pass by'" (v. 11a).

And then this happens:

> Then a great and powerful wind tore the mountains apart and shattered the rocks before the LORD, but the LORD was not in the wind. After the wind there was an earthquake, but the LORD was not in the earthquake. After the earthquake came a fire, but the LORD was not in the fire. And after the fire came a gentle whisper. When Elijah heard it, he pulled his cloak over his face and went out and stood at the mouth of the cave. (vv. 11b–13a)

And then, whispering this time, God asks the question again: "Then a voice said to him, 'What are you doing here, Elijah?'" (v. 13b).

I love the subtlety of how he puts Elijah's name at the end of the question rather than at the beginning. God is gentle like that. Now, you won't believe this (or maybe you will),

Elijah gives the *exact same answer*, which was not an answer. In the immortal words of the great prophet of baseball, Yogi Berra, "It's like dejá vu—all over again."

> He replied, "I have been very zealous for the Lord God Almighty. The Israelites have rejected your covenant, torn down your altars, and put your prophets to death with the sword. I am the only one left, and now they are trying to kill me too." (v. 14)

And then the question comes to me, "What are you doing here, John David?" It is much easier to recount my circumstances and rehash my challenges. It is much harder to actually answer the question, "What are you doing here?"

So what are you doing here, (insert your name)? I'll go first.

I am waking up to the rest of my life. At fifty-five, maybe I have a year. Maybe I have fifty. Whatever it is, I am waking up to the sheer possibility of what Jesus can do with, for, in, and through my life. That said, I am renouncing any and all grandiosity of my former narcissistic ambitions to do something great for God. I am sowing for a great awakening. To that end, I am becoming small, like a seed. I have given up on the Republicans and the Democrats and this cause or that so-called movement and all the other broken ideologies to fix things. Only one kingdom will endure and prevail, the kingdom of Jesus, and this kingdom is hovering just over the present state of chaos, already breaking in through the tiniest seeds that will become—and indeed are becoming—the tallest trees. What am I doing here? I am learning day by day the difference between being in the world "for Christ" and being "in Christ" for the world. And I'm trying to encourage as many people as I can, every single day, that we are coming to the end of a long season of slumber, that it is time to wake up and rise from the dead, that Jesus is now shining, revealing himself far beyond anything that we ever knew or imagined him to be before. He will take anybody who will raise their hand. I am just one of his scouts, one of his ambassadors, looking to field a team; looking for raised hands ready to be filled with miracle seeds. That's what I'm doing here. And as the old-time evangelists are wont to say, "I see that hand!"

The Prayer

Yes, Lord, thank you for the questions you ask in your Word, when you know the answer all along. Thank you for this question, "What are you doing here?" Thank you for making it personal to us. Thank you for helping us to actually answer it; to get past rehashing all our circumstances and pain and all the stuff you already know. Show us what we are doing here. Thank you for showing us it doesn't need to be some grand thing but ordinary and real. Holy Spirit, show us the potency of your possibilities in our ordinary and very real lies, right here and right now. In Jesus' name, amen.

The Question

- What are you doing here, (insert your name)?

When the Word of God Asks Us a Question (Question 3 of 3)

MARK 10:51 | "What do you want me to do for you?" Jesus asked him.

Consider This

There is a sense in which I always want to begin with Question #3.

"What do you want me to do for you?" Jesus asked him.

There is a larger sense in which one must first answer Question #1 and Question #2.

Where are you? And, what are you doing here?

So much to talk about with today's text. Let's begin with the one to whom Jesus asks the question, Bartimaeus, a.k.a. Blind Bartimaeus.

> Then they came to Jericho. As Jesus and his disciples, together with a large crowd, were leaving the city, a blind man, Bartimaeus (which means "son of Timaeus"), was sitting by the roadside begging. When he heard that it was Jesus of Nazareth, he began to shout, "Jesus, Son of David, have mercy on me!" (Mark 10:46–47)

Bartimaeus—a poor, blind, and broken son—sits by the roadside begging. We are in the large entourage of Jesus, on our way out of Jericho, about to get on that treacherous road en route to Jerusalem. Everyone thinks we are headed for the take-down of Rome and the exaltation of Jesus. He will be lifted up all right, in a way we never imagined, nailed to a cross.

Bartimaeus couldn't see Jesus, but he heard it was him. It is doubtful that Jesus could see Bartimaeus, but we know he heard him. Bartimaeus was shouting, as loud as he could, "Jesus, Son of David, have mercy on me!" He shouted so loud we get this:

Many rebuked him and told him to be quiet, but he shouted all the more, "Son of David, have mercy on me!"

Bartimaeus knew the answer to Question #1, "Where are you?" He knew the answer to Question #2, "What are you doing here?" And as a result, he knew the answer to Question #3, "What do you want me to do for you?" "Have mercy on me!" he shouted.

It's fascinating to back up on the road a few miles and revisit the conversation between James and John and Jesus.

> Then James and John, the sons of Zebedee, came to him. "Teacher," they said, "we want you to do for us whatever we ask."
>
> "What do you want me to do for you?" he asked.
>
> They replied, "Let one of us sit at your right and the other at your left in your glory." (vv. 35–37)

Same question. Different guys. Way different answer.

Back up another click and parents are bringing their children to Jesus asking for blessing. Back up another click and a rich man is asking Jesus for eternal life. Back up another click and he is telling the story of a widow in front a wicked judge asking for justice. Jesus, in one way or another, is asking every single person in the world this question: *What do you want me to do for you?*

Only a person whose eyes have been opened to where they really are and what they are really doing there is aware of the true state of their real condition. Go back and read the text, and while you are at it read Luke's telling in chapter 18. The true state and real condition of the human race (whether they know it or not) can be brought down to one word: *desperation*. The rich have enough money to cover it up, until they don't. The Pharisees down at First Baptist and Lost Methodist have enough respectability in the community to hide their desperation, until they can't. But the poor, and the children, and the lepers, and the sick, and the blind—they can't hide it. That's why Jesus calls them "blessed." So must we become those things in order to get the answer to the question right? No, we need only come to the ever-deepening realization of our own desperation and respond to his question from that place of honest sobriety.

It's interesting. Bartimaeus, an impoverished beggar, did not ask Jesus for money. Because he knew where he was and what he was doing there and who he was asking, he knew exactly what he wanted. He needed money. He wanted something money couldn't buy.

I want to see.

Now watch what happens.

"Go," said Jesus, "your faith has healed you." Immediately he received his sight and followed Jesus along the road.

So Jesus, the Word made flesh, asking, "What do you want me to do for you?"

Okay, I'll go first.

Lord Jesus, I want your joy to be in me and my joy to be complete (John 15:11).

Your turn.

The Prayer

Yes, Lord, thank you for asking. Holy Spirit, help us answer in a way worthy of the question and the one asking. In Jesus' name, amen.

The Question

- So why is it that we tend to ask Jesus for more of what we already have and don't feel like we have enough of—as though more of what is not working or satisfying would somehow do the trick?

THE SOWER'S CREED

Today,
I sow for a great awakening.

Today,
I stake everything on the promise of the Word of God.
I depend entirely on the power of the Holy Spirit.
I have the same mind in me that was in Christ Jesus.
Because Jesus is good news and Jesus is in me,
I am good news.

Today,
I will sow the extravagance of the gospel
everywhere I go and into everyone I meet.

Today,
I will love others as Jesus has loved me.

Today,
I will remember that the tiniest seeds become the
tallest trees; that the seeds of today become the shade
of tomorrow; that the faith of right now becomes
the future of the everlasting kingdom.

Today,
I sow for a great awakening.

Printed by Libri Plureos GmbH in Hamburg, Germany